# DISCOURAGED?...

## In the midst of it all,
## God is in control

Rob & Lisa Laizure

Discouraged?
In the midst of it all, God is in control.

By Rob & Lisa Laizure

Copyright © 2011 by Rob and Lisa Laizure
Revised 2014

Printed in the United States

ISBN 978-0-9819065-7-7

Unless otherwise indicated, all scripture verses are from:
Copyright © 1992-2011 Logos Bible Software.

The Holy Bible, Libronix NASB Version

ConnectingTheDotsMinistries.com

Rob and Lisa Laizure have authored several other books:

*Connecting the Dots*

*Growing Faith*

*One Way*

*Teamwork*

*The Holy Land*

*The Truth About Marriage*

*True or False*

# Table of Contents

# CHAPTER 1

# *Be Encouraged*

A few years ago at Bible Study, we handed out a book called *The Kingdom Assignment* written by Denny and Leesa Bellesi. Here was the challenge they gave their congregation:

*If you accept the assignment, you will take a small amount of money and increase it up to a hundredfold or more. You will have the means to help countless people—some with food and clothing, others with medicine or the gospel message—and in the process, no matter how much money your investment turns into, no matter how many people you will help, you will walk away with more than what your investment will ever make and more than those you've invested in.[i]*

It was amazing how inventive people became. Some people bought books for lonely people, blankets for the homeless, and care packages and food for the hungry. Some bought Bibles for others and helped build homes in Mexico. The book was so incredible because it was a challenge to do what God has called all of us to do: serve others.

After the girls in Bible Study read the book, one came to me a few weeks later and said she was so frustrated after reading it that she threw it across the room—not exactly the response we were hoping for! She explained she was just tired: tired of always feeling she had to do more and tired of feeling she was not doing enough. She was a young mother with young children. She was tired from lack of sleep and from all that goes along with a busy life.

Have you ever felt that way? Have you ever felt physically exhausted from:

- Working hard during the week,
- Coaching your son's Little League team,
- Raising your children,
- Cooking and cleaning,
- Going to Bible Study,
- Going to small group,
- Fixing meals for those who are sick,
- Mowing the lawn for an injured neighbor,

Have you ever felt emotionally exhausted from:

- Trying to read your Bible daily,
- Trying to pray without ceasing,
- Trying to only say things that would please God,
- Trying to witness to everyone you meet,
- Trying to distinguish the voice of God from the rest of the noise,
- Trying to make sure your children are taught God's Word,
- Trying to be loving, kind, and forgiving,
- Trying to keep God in focus every moment?

If so, this book is for you. We decided to write this book after I (Rob) spoke to a man who said he felt as if he was in a desert; God was nowhere to be found. He was reading his Bible, praying, and sharing the Gospel, yet he was discouraged. God didn't seem to care about Him anymore, which begs the question: Why? Why do we go through times like this in our lives when God feels so distant? A man in our small group said he had been feeling so emotionally exhausted he hadn't felt the joy of the Lord in years.

How is that possible? How can we be discouraged when God is living in our lives?

One summer, I (Lisa) went through months of discouragement and depression. I felt as though God disappeared out of my life. I was tired of going to church, even though I know how vital it is to my life. I was tired of telling everyone God was in control when I felt my world was spinning out of control. I was tired of hearing people say God was speaking to them while I wondered why He wasn't speaking to me. I was tired of other religions and the people who came into my life who were convinced they were right and I was wrong. Frankly, I was tired of it all.

In the midst of my discouragement, some friends called us on vacation, and we met them for breakfast. As we were talking, our friend said he could sense a hint of "spiritual exhaustion." As we talked, we told them what I was going through, only to hear his wife, who was in tears, saying she had been feeling the same way. It made us realize that many people feel discouraged in their Christian walk, but many of us are not honest enough to admit it. We feel we have to put on a smile, never be sad, never question our faith, and hold our doubts and confusion in. I for one could not do that anymore.

This black cloud hanging over me did not want to leave. I didn't want to read my Bible, I couldn't pray because I was sure God wasn't listening, and I didn't care to share this faith that didn't seem to be working for me. I felt hopeless for the first time in my life. I felt if I died I would never see heaven. I felt I could never teach another Bible study because I had nothing to offer. The world felt hopeless, the stock market was falling, our businesses were struggling, and my trust in the God who held it all together had evaporated.

One night, I was sitting on the balcony watching the ocean. With tears streaming down my face for no reason whatsoever except a sense my life would never be the same, my son came out and sat with me. He told me that it was okay; all Christians go through times like these and all Christians face times of darkness. He talked with me, prayed for me, and encouraged me. I knew he was right but I told him I could not pull myself out of this—only God could in His timing. For whatever reason, I was in this dark place, and my only hope was Him.

The next morning, I decided to pick up my Bible and in God's grace and perfect timing, I happened to read **Micah 7:7-8: "But as for me, I will watch expectantly for the Lord; I will wait for the God of my salvation. My God will hear me. Do not rejoice over me, O my enemy. Though I fall I will rise; though I dwell in darkness, the Lord is a light for me."** I looked up at Rob, once again in tears, but this time for a good reason: I knew God placed that verse there for me. Even though I knew I had been falling into a deep dark hole, there was hope that I would rise again. Even though I was dwelling in darkness, the Lord would be my light. The second half of **Micah 7:9** says this: **"Until He pleads my case and executes justice for me. He will bring me out to the light, and I will see His righteousness."** I couldn't do anything—He had to do it all, and for the first time in a long time, I felt the darkness lift.

If you feel anything like this "spiritual exhaustion" we have been talking about, here is some encouragement: *you are not alone*. From Genesis to Revelation, we see many discouraged people in the Bible: Abraham, Moses, Joseph, Job, David, Paul and Peter, just to name a few. These are big names, men who loved God passionately and devoted themselves wholeheartedly to Him. And guess what? They felt discouraged, they felt abandoned at times, and they felt fearful… *just like many of us*. What they learned to do was counter those discouraging feelings with the truth about God and His Word. Hopefully, we will learn the same.

Many Christians are discouraged, and our hope and prayer for this book is that when you are done reading it, you will be *encouraged*. When we come to Jesus in repentance and faith, we often assume our lives will be great all the time. We assume we shouldn't have many problems, and if we do, they should always turn out to benefit us. When they don't, we do not know how to process that. Many people walk away from their faith or walk through life in a daze, wondering where God is in it all. Many people wake up each day trying to just "make it through." Is that how you feel? Is that how we *should* feel?

Are you worried all the time that God is mad at you? Are you tired of constantly feeling like you can never do enough to earn favor with Him? Are you emotionally exhausted because of sin that you can't seem to get a handle on? Do you feel overwhelmed with guilt if you miss a Bible study or miss church? Are you sure that God is displeased with you because you "messed up" once again? Do you feel you cannot make a move without knowing whether that is what God wants you to do? Do you keep a list of rules and regulations and try to live by them? What happens when you say "no" to a project at church? How do you think God feels about that? Are you guilt-ridden, and tired of trying to work harder to make God love you? Is that the life that Jesus promised when He said in **John 10:10, "The thief comes only to steal and kill and destroy; I came that they may have life, and have it abundantly."**

Maybe you are not discouraged because of emotional or spiritual exhaustion. Maybe you are discouraged and depressed because of a tragedy that has come into your life. Driving home one night, we were surprised to see the main road leading to our house closed down. As we drove up to a police officer, we rolled down our window and asked what the problem was. He told us there had been a car accident, and it would be a while before the road was open again.

The next few days told us the story of what happened: A mother and father, along with their two children (4 years old and 6 months old), were looking for property in hopes of moving their children out where there was more land. As they stopped to make a left hand turn, a truck driven by a young driver was coming up behind them at a fast speed. The driver of this truck said he never saw the car that was waiting to make its turn. What happened was disaster and complete heartache. The baby died, the 4-year-old had numerous, serious injuries, and the parents were left completely devastated. How could this happen? Where was God? Didn't He know how much they loved their children? Doesn't He know what something like this does to a parent's hopes, plans, and desires?

In your life, maybe it isn't something so tragic, but it is just as devastating. Maybe your spouse walked out the door. Maybe your child is on drugs. Maybe your daughter is unwed and pregnant. Maybe you lost your job. Maybe your business went under. Whatever the problems may be, where do you find comfort? Where do you go when your world seems to be falling apart? Where do you turn when there seem to be no answers?

Many people turn to their friends and family or to psychologists and psychiatrists. Some turn to drugs and alcohol. Some just run away to another state. Some join a religion, and others walk away from religion. Some pour themselves into their work; others sit in front of the television, never really able to get on with their lives.

Let's face it: we live in a world of confusion and fear. All we need to do is turn on our television sets at night to see the fear. Will there be war? What will happen in Iraq? What will Iran do? Will the United States be attacked? Where will it be? Airplane? Train? Car bomb? Will I be there? What about our children? What kind of world will our grandchildren live in? What about the elections? Who will be President? Will the country go under? Will we lose our home, our job, or our health? What will happen to us? Fear is a gripping emotion, yet with all that is going on, we can assure you of the one thing that we can count on:

## *God is still on His throne, and He is still in complete control.*

If you are reading this and you are a Christian, you should be comforted by the fact that the God in whom you place your trust, your life, your job, and your children, is never out of control.

You trust a merciful, loving God who promises in **Romans 8:28** that He **"...causes all things to work together for good to those who love God, to those who are called according to His purpose."** How does a death, a sickness, or a job loss work for good? How does a painful divorce, an unhappy marriage, or a wayward child work for good? *God alone knows the answer to those questions.* He promises all that is happening to you is conforming you to the image of Jesus, that through all the heartache and disappointments, He is growing you up to look more like Him.

If you are reading this and you have never committed your life to the Lord Jesus Christ, you cannot claim anything that happens to you will work for good. You cannot go to bed at night free from worry because you have never trusted your life to the One who holds the key to life and death. You do not get to claim the same promises of God that His children get to claim. True comfort can only be claimed by those who, by faith, have a personal relationship with God through His Son Jesus.

Our son played college football, and one night at his game we saw something interesting. Some of the coaches were up in the sky box where they could see things from a higher vantage point. Throughout the game, a coach on the field gave the headphones to some of the players so that the coaches in the sky box could tell them how to play the game even better. The coaches could see things the players on the field could not see.

That is how our Christian life works: God is in heaven and is speaking to us—not through headphones but through the Holy Spirit who lives inside of us. He is coaching us on how to live life, He is comforting us in the hard times, and He is helping us persevere to the end. He uses His Word, the Bible, to help us play this game of life, and as in our son's football game, the players had to listen to the coaches in the sky box. The same is true for us: our best bet is to listen to and obey the God of this universe who is letting us know the best way to play this game of life.

Does that mean we will always get what we want? Does that mean things will always go our way? Does that mean the bad in life will never touch us? Does that mean tragedy will never strike our families or friends? In the Bible, a man named David knew trouble, heartache, deception, grief, hurt, and disappointment more than most could imagine. He was supposed to be King, yet the current King was jealous and tried to kill him. He spent many years of his life on the run. His baby died. His oldest son tried to take away his throne and died in the process. His one and only true friend died in battle. He spent years and years fighting for his country. He wanted to build a temple for God, and God said "no." He was loved and adored by those in Israel, but along with that adoration came unimaginable heartache. Where did he turn? Where did he go to get the comfort he needed in those troubled times?

King David recognized that heartache, fear, and desperation are part of living on this earth. His responses to these battles have been written down for us in the book of Psalms in the Bible. He battled his fears with his *knowledge of God*. He battled uncertainties in life with his *devotion to God*. The more he grew in his faith, the more he learned how to trust his God. The more he hurt, the more he trusted.

Looking back at the life of David, whom God called "a man after His own heart," we can be assured that this life will be full of trials and difficulties. Yet David understood that God was his rock and his source of strength through it all. Because of David's relationship with God, he tried to look at life with an eternal viewpoint. The things that David went through give us hope and comfort for the things we are going through. His responses to God help us to learn how we should respond.

Please join us as we take a journey through the Bible to see how other Christians handled discouragement. The Bible has the answers we need to live a peaceful and joyful life, even in the midst of trouble. We need to open up His Word on a daily basis to allow God to speak to us, which He does through the Bible. As

Christians, we have the Holy Spirit who is God living inside of us. Think about that: God lives *inside of us!* It is up to Him to comfort us and remind us that He has never lost control of this world or our lives. Once we get to know the true God of the Bible, we can be assured that our lives are in good hands and that He will take care of us.

Let's take a look at those who went before us and see how we can learn to live a joyful, abundant life, just like they learned to do.

# CHAPTER 2

# *Job*
## *Discouragement When My World Falls Apart*

As Christians, we should be joyful in all things, yet many times we are not. We let life get to us; we allow circumstances to rule over our feelings. Sometimes we feel like a black cloud is following us. Nothing is going right and we cannot make sense of the things that are happening. Maybe your children have walked away from the Lord, or maybe your business is going under. Maybe you are losing your home because of the economy, or maybe you just found out you have cancer. All these things and many others contribute to the feeling of dark clouds and gray skies following you everywhere you go.

All through the Bible, others have felt the same way. Take Job for instance. He was a righteous man who loved and served God all of his days. The Bible says this in **Job 1:1-3:**

> **"There was a man in the land of Uz whose name was Job; and that man was blameless, upright, fearing God and turning away from evil. Seven sons and three daughters were born to him. His possessions also were 7,000 sheep, 3,000 camels, 500 yoke of oxen, 500 female donkeys, and very many servants; and that man was the greatest of all the men of the east."**

One day his entire world turned upside down. His 10 children all died in a freak accident where the house they were in collapsed because of a wind storm, his sheep and servants were killed by fire from heaven, and on top of that, thieves stole his camels and killed the rest of his servants. I don't know about you, but for us that would rank pretty high on the "bad day" chart. As if that wasn't enough, after all of this happened, Job lost his health and was covered in boils.

Amazingly, Job started worshiping God, even in his tragedy:

**"Then Job arose and tore his robe and shaved his head, and he fell to the ground and worshiped. He said, 'Naked I came from my mother's womb, and naked I shall return there. The Lord gave and the Lord has taken away. Blessed be the name of the Lord.' Through all this Job did not sin nor did he blame God." (Job 1:20-22)**

Job is our hero because we are not sure our reaction would be the same as his. We hope it would, but when something simple happens, like our air conditioning goes out, we usually don't have "the Lord gave and the Lord takes away" kind of attitude. But Job seemed to trust God no matter what.

However, in Job 3, Job started getting frustrated. He never cursed or blamed God, but he did start getting discouraged. **Job 3:1-6 says, "Afterward Job opened his mouth and cursed the day of his birth. And Job said, 'Let the day perish on which I was to be born, and the night which said, 'A boy is conceived'. May that day be darkness; let not God above care for it, nor light shine on it. Let darkness and black gloom claim it; let a cloud settle on it; let the blackness of the day terrify it. As for that night, let darkness seize it; let it not rejoice among the days of the year; let it not come into the number of the months.'"**

Job asked another question in verses 11 and 12: **"Why did I not die at birth, come forth from the womb and expire? Why did the knees receive me, and why the breasts, that I should suck?"** Have you ever been discouraged enough to wonder the same thing? Why am I alive? Why was I ever born? What is the purpose for my life and the difficulties I am facing? Why would you do this to me God? Why would You allow the pain in my life if you loved me? Why?

Most questions that begin with the word "why" usually do not have an answer. Our questions should always begin with the word "who." The answer will always be God, and He will always have a purpose behind what happens in our lives, which is to make us more like Jesus. The problem is that this side of heaven, most of the time we will never know the "why," but we can know and trust the "Who." The interesting thing about Job is that he had some friends who wanted to "help" him get through this, yet they gave him advice that did not line up with God's character. They tried to help Job figure out why bad things were happening in his life. Could it be sin? Could it be self-righteousness? It *has* to be something, they seemed to conclude. Yet in God's perfect timing, He decided to speak to Job Himself, and what Job heard was shocking. Never were Job's "why" questions answered, but Job's "Who" question was made perfectly clear.

**Job 38:1-3** reads, **"Then the Lord answered Job out of the whirlwind and said, 'Who is this that darkens counsel by words without knowledge? Now gird up your loins like a man, and I will ask you, and you instruct Me!'"** God was not too thrilled with the counsel of Job's friends because they gave answers without knowledge, so God began asking Job questions! By the end of four chapters of questions from God, Job began to see that God was God and he was not. This world and everything in it is His. He does what He pleases for His own purposes. Here are some of the questions God asked Job:

> **"Where were you when I laid the foundation of the earth? Tell Me, if you have**

> understanding, who set its measurements?
> Since you know. Or who stretched the line
> on it? On what were its bases sunk? Or who
> laid its cornerstone, when the morning
> stars sang together and all the sons of God
> shouted for joy?" (Job 38:4-7)

Since Job was nowhere to be found when God laid the foundation of the earth, should he question God? Isn't He the Creator? If Job wasn't consulted by God on how to form the earth, why should Job question any of his circumstances? It seems as if God was trying to show Job that He does what He wants. He is Creator and Sustainer.

> "Or who enclosed the sea with doors when,
> bursting forth, it went out from the womb;
> When I made a cloud its garment and thick
> darkness its swaddling band, and I placed
> boundaries on it and set a bolt and doors,
> and I said, 'Thus far you shall come, but
> no farther; and here shall your proud waves
> stop?'" (Job 38:8-11)

God then started asking Job about the ocean. Not only did God create the foundation of the earth, but He also wanted Job to understand that everything is under His control, even the place where the waves stop. When we were in San Diego a couple of years ago, we were looking at the waves and thinking of this verse. With the ocean being as big as it is, why does it always stop where it does? Why doesn't it empty miles inland? We would say it is because God is big and awesome and completely in control of everything that happens.

Here are some more questions that God asked Job:

> "Where is the way to the dwelling of light?
> And darkness, where is its place, that you

may take it to its territory and that you may discern the paths to its home?" (Job 38:19-20)

"Have you entered the storehouses of the snow, or have you seen the storehouses of the hail, which I have reserved for the time of distress, for the day of war and battle?" (Job 38:22-23)

"Can you bind the chains of the Pleiades, or loose the cords of Orion? Can you lead forth a constellation in its season, and guide the Bear with her satellites? Do you know the ordinances of the heavens, or fix their rule over the earth?" (Job 38:31-33)

"Do you know the time the mountain goats give birth? Do you observe the calving of the deer? Can you count the months they fulfill, or do you know the time they give birth? They kneel down, they bring forth their young, they get rid of their labor pains. Their offspring become strong, they grow up in the open field; they leave and do not return to them." (Job 39:1-4)

In the middle of this questioning, God challenged Job to answer these questions: **"Then the Lord said to Job, 'Will the faultfinder contend with the Almighty? Let him who reproves God answer it.'" (Job 40:1-2)** In his study Bible notes, John MacArthur says this about these verses:

*God challenged Job to answer all the questions he had posed. God didn't need to know the answer, but Job needed to admit his weakness, inferiority, and inability to even try to figure out God's infinite mind. God's wisdom was so superior, His sovereign control of everything so complete, that this was all Job needed to know.*[ii]

The more we understand God controls everything, the more we can then rest in the fact that even our bad circumstances are allowed by Him. Even though Job never got the answers he wanted, he did begin to recognize God for who He is. Job's response to God in the first series of questions in **Job 40:4-5** says, **"Behold, I am insignificant; what can I reply to You? I lay my hand on my mouth. Once I have spoken, and I will not answer; even twice, and I will add nothing more."** Once we begin to see how insignificant we are and how incredible God is, only then can we deal with life the way it should be dealt with. We have to look at all of our problems, trials, hurts, and pain with an eternal point of view. What is God trying to teach us? Are the things of this world more important than Him? Do we trust ourselves or God with our problems? How would we ever know the answer to any of these questions if we didn't go through hard times?

When we find ourselves with a dark cloud hanging over us, most of the time it is because we are looking inward and not upward. We focus on our problems, we focus on our circumstances, and we feel sorry for ourselves. Christ has promised us incredible joy, yet we become so self absorbed that we can't see Him in anything. Think of this: can God solve your problem? Can He bring your wayward child back home? Can He save your struggling marriage? Can He help you through your financial troubles? Can He bring salvation to your household? Can He?

Ask Job, and you will hear him say again what he did in **Job 42:2-6**:

> **"I know that You can do all things, and that no purpose of Yours can be thwarted. 'Who is this that hides counsel without knowledge?' Therefore I have declared that which I did not understand, things too wonderful for me, which I did not know. 'Hear, now, and I will speak; I will ask You, and You instruct me.' I have heard of You by**

**the hearing of the ear; but now my eye sees You; therefore I retract, and I repent in dust and ashes."**

Job finally got it: God can do anything. Nothing that God has a purpose for can be thwarted. God is God, and Job had to learn to trust Him. Does that mean everything will always turn out like we want? Job would probably say losing his children, wealth, and health was not what he wanted in life. But once Job saw God for who He is, he was able to accept God's plan for his life.

The same should be true for us. Do we have financial problems? We should smile, knowing God is going to teach us something incredible. Do we have marital problems? We should be thankful, knowing God can restore anything. Is our child far from home? We should relax, knowing God sees everything that is going on. That is why we do not have to live under a dark black cloud of dicsouragement. That is why when we have days that seem gray, we should look upward past the dark cloud and see the sun really is shining. Life becomes clear when we focus on the greatness of Him who holds everything in place. When things seem to be falling apart, just as they did in Job's life, we need to grab hold of the truth of God's Word: **"Who has given to Me that I should repay him? Whatever is under the whole heaven is Mine." (Job 41:11)**

There is no need to be sad or depressed when we know who holds the key to our future. God always has a purpose and a plan for everything He does, even if it is hard for us to see. Stand on scriptures like **Isaiah 14:24: "The Lord of hosts has sworn saying, 'Surely, just as I have intended so it has happened, and just as I have planned so it will stand...'"** The world is not reeling out of control, and neither is your life, if you are His child. As Christians, we have to grasp the fact He loves us more than anything. That does not always mean a pain-free life, as Job quickly found out. Even very righteous people who love God with all their hearts have serious problems. The difference is living life under a dark cloud or living life above that cloud. The choice is ours.

If you cannot seem to get your focus off of yourself, remember the Holy Spirit who lives inside of you is the only One who can change your perspective in life. He is the only One who can give you peace and joy in situations that seem helpless and hopeless. You need to ask. Ask Him to remove the cloud. Ask Him to give you the desire you need to trust Him. As we attach ourselves to Christ and read His Word to get to know Him, we will start seeing life through eternal lenses. We will look at life through His viewpoint instead of ours. That is cause in itself to rejoice. The more we know Him, the more we can deal with whatever comes our way.

> **"The Lord restored the fortunes of Job when he prayed for his friends, and the Lord increased all that Job had twofold. Then all his brothers and all his sisters and all who had known him before came to him, and they ate bread with him in his house; and they consoled him and comforted him for all the adversities that the Lord had brought on him. And each one gave him one piece of money, and each a ring of gold. The Lord blessed the latter days of Job more than his beginning; and he had 14,000 sheep and 6,000 camels and 1,000 yoke of oxen and 1,000 female donkeys. He had seven sons and three daughters. He named the first Jemimah, and the second Keziah, and the third Keren-happuch. In all the land no women were found so fair as Job's daughters; and their father gave them inheritance among their brothers. After this, Job lived 140 years, and saw his sons and his grandsons, four generations. And Job died, an old man and full of days." (Job 42:10-17)**

Sometimes heartache is just what we need to see God for who He is. In the life of Job, as discouraged and confused as he was, it ended well. Once he learned who he was in comparison to God, God restored his fortunes and his family. That does not always happen, but either way we believe Job would have been content, for he had finally seen God. Once that happens in a person's life, earthly things do not really matter much.

Here is a serious problem that many of us face:

*We don't have the faith to believe any of this.*

The great thing about God is He understands we are human, so faith has to be something that is given to us. **Mark 9:20-24** shows that we need to cry out to Jesus when we don't have the faith or belief to trust Him:

> **"They brought the boy to Him. When he saw Him, immediately the spirit threw him into a convulsion, and falling to the ground, he began rolling around and foaming at the mouth. And He asked his father, 'How long has this been happening to him?' And he said, 'From childhood. It has often thrown him both into the fire and into the water to destroy him. But if You can do anything, take pity on us and help us!' And Jesus said to him, 'If You can? All things are possible to him who believes.' Immediately the boy's father cried out and said, 'I do believe; help my unbelief.'"**

Don't we all do this when things don't go our way? Don't we say things like…

God, *if you can*…will you save my marriage?
God, *if you can*…will you save our business?
God, *if you can*…will you get me a job?
God, *if you can*…will you bring my wayward
    child home?

God, *if you can*…will you make sure my children come
to saving faith in You?

We can imagine Him looking at this father in Mark 9 and
thinking,

"I created this world,
I flung the stars in the heavens,
I made the sun, the moon and stars and created
the galaxies,
I made the oceans and the rivers,
I made the lion and giraffe,
I control the wind, the rain, and the snow,
I am God."

**"*If* You can?" Of course He can! He is God!**

He never got mad at this father; instead, He reassured him.
He told him that anything was possible if only he would believe.
Therein lies the problem: sometimes we don't believe. We don't
believe He will step in and comfort us; we don't believe He will
do as He promised. We doubt His existence, we doubt His Word,
and we doubt He really cares. This father did exactly what we
have to do in times of doubt and discouragement: *we have to be
honest with God.* We have to tell Him we don't have the faith
needed to trust Him. We have to ask Him to give us the faith to
trust Him in the difficult times. Nowhere does the Bible promise
He will say yes to all we ask for, but He does promise to see us
through the difficult times. When we struggle, we need to ask
Him to help us in our unbelief and then wait. It is amazing what
happens when we, just like Job, come to Him empty handed,
honest, humble, and scared. He shows up.

**And when He does, our lives are never the same.**

# CHAPTER 3

# *Joseph*
# *Discouragement As We*
# *Wonder, "Where is God?"*

Do you ever feel God has disappeared out of your life? Do you ever feel your circumstances are so out of control that He could not possibly be paying attention? Do you ever wonder why your prayers seem to bounce off the ceiling and you are convinced He must have gone on vacation? Why are you unemployed when you are desperately seeking to work? Why is your child still far from God when you have prayed for him for years and years? Why has your house not sold when God knows your desperate situation? Why doesn't your husband or wife love you any more even though you have prayed and prayed for your relationship to grow? Why does your world seem to be falling apart? WHERE IS GOD?

Sound familiar? What makes this situation more difficult is the fact you know you are living a godly life. You are going to church, serving God, sharing Him with others, and giving of your time and treasures, yet God doesn't seem to be appreciating all your hard work. Isn't that an easy trap to fall into? We do good things for God, and in return, we expect good things back! But is that how God works? Is that the kind of relationship we have with Him?

Let's read about the life of Joseph in the Bible. He was the second to youngest of 12 children, and his dad seemed to love him more than the rest. Because of his brothers' jealousy, they devised a plan to sell Joseph to foreigners and tell their father he had been killed. How frightening for Joseph who was a young boy of 16 or 17. Suddenly ripped from his family and the comfort of his home, he was now transported to a foreign country and sold as a slave. How tragic that would be for anyone, let alone a young boy.

> **"So it came about, when Joseph reached his brothers, that they stripped Joseph of his tunic, the varicolored tunic that was on him; and they took him and threw him into the pit. Now the pit was empty, without any water in it. Then they sat down to eat a meal. And as they raised their eyes and looked, behold, a caravan of Ishmaelites was coming from Gilead, with their camels bearing aromatic gum and balm and myrrh, on their way to bring them down to Egypt. Judah said to his brothers, 'What profit is it for us to kill our brother and cover up his blood? Come and let us sell him to the Ishmaelites and not lay our hands on him, for he is our brother, our own flesh.' And his brothers listened to him. Then some Midianite traders passed by, so they pulled him up and lifted Joseph out of the pit, and sold him to the Ishmaelites for twenty shekels of silver. Thus they brought Joseph into Egypt." (Genesis 37:23–28)**

Joseph was now in Egypt, and he must have been terrified. The young boy whom his father loved and doted on was now going to be a slave. Think of what must have been going through his mind: "Will I be hurt? Will my father come looking for me? Will I ever get out of here? Will my brothers feel bad, come back, and tell me they were just joking?" All of these things must have been going through his mind as he was trying to deal with the turn his life had taken.

Now fast forward to your life. Has your life taken such a drastic turn that you are confused? Have you lost the job you thought you would retire from? Has your spouse walked out the door, even though he or she promised to love and cherish you forever? Has a sickness or disease invaded your body? Has someone close to you passed away? All of these events and Joseph's situation can both be discouraging and frightening. Yet Joseph somehow began to recognize God was with him—even in those times of confusion.

> "Now Joseph had been taken down to Egypt; and Potiphar, an Egyptian officer of Pharaoh, the captain of the bodyguard, bought him from the Ishmaelites, who had taken him down there. The Lord was with Joseph, so he became a successful man. And he was in the house of his master, the Egyptian. Now his master saw that the Lord was with him and how the Lord caused all that he did to prosper in his hand. So Joseph found favor in his sight and became his personal servant; and he made him overseer over his house, and all that he owned he put in his charge. It came about that from the time he made him overseer in his house and over all that he owned, the Lord blessed the Egyptian's house on account of Joseph; thus the Lord's blessing was upon all that he owned, in the house and in the field. So he left everything he owned in Joseph's charge; and with him there he did not concern himself with anything except the food which he ate. Now Joseph was handsome in form and appearance." (Genesis 39:1-6)

Instead of being tortured, starved, and put to hard labor, Joseph became a very successful slave. Even though his world was turned upside down, it seems he started to recognize God was in his difficult situations after all. I (Lisa) remember a very difficult time in our lives when a song came out on the radio called "In It After All" by Larnelle Harris. Joseph somehow seems to understand, just like Larnelle Harris writes about, that God was with him even in his pain and heartache.

### "In It After All" Lyrics

*So You were in it after all*
*All of those moments I spent crying*
*When something inside of me was dying*
*I didn't know that You heard me*
*Each time I called*
*You had a reason for those trials*
*It seems I grew stronger every mile*
*Now I know You were in it after all*

*We're always ready Lord to take the glory*
*But we're seldom willing to endure the pain*
*You were with me when the sun was shining,*
*And You were still beside me when it rained*

*So You were in it after all*
*Taking the blows that I'd been given*
*Mending the wounds that needed mending*
*I didn't know that You heard me each time I called*
*I guess it's easy now to see it,*
*I don't know how I could have missed it Jesus*
*But You were in it after all*

If we think God has abandoned us during difficult times, we can get depressed and discouraged; however, Joseph seemed to flourish instead of feeling sorry for himself. He seemed to have a great and high view of God. Would he rather have his old, comfortable life back? Probably. But somehow, God does more in our lives when He puts us to the test, and hopefully, just like Joseph, we will come out on the other side refined.

If only we could look at everything that comes into our lives through eternal lenses. If only we could recognize that through all the pain, sorrow, and confusion we experience, God really is in it with us. Grasping the fact that the God of the Universe lives inside of us and is working behind the scenes in all that happens in our lives, is a comfort.

The great thing about the story of Joseph is that he prospered in a bad situation. The problem is that many times in our own lives, we do not seem to be prospering. The bills are piling up, our marriage seems to be falling apart, our health seems to be disintegrating, and nobody is hiring for the job we so desperately need. What do we do then? How can we not get discouraged?

The Bible is so incredible because it is honest about the reality of life on earth. Instead of allowing us to think Joseph flourished without any problems, the Bible teaches us that even when someone does the right thing, it can still mean trouble. The story of Joseph reminds us life can take twists and turns we would rather not go through. As we will see, Joseph went to prison for doing all the right things:

- Being honest
- Having integrity
- Loving God more than pleasure

Shouldn't God honor those qualities? Shouldn't God honor the fact we read our Bibles and go to church? Shouldn't He heal our afflictions, give us the job we want, and make our spouse love us? Why do we have to suffer and go through hard times? Life doesn't seem fair to us sometimes and it was just about to get really unfair for Joseph:

**"It came about after these events that his master's wife looked with desire at Joseph,**

and she said, 'Lie with me.' But he refused
and said to his master's wife, 'Behold, with
me here, my master does not concern
himself with anything in the house, and he
has put all that he owns in my charge. There
is no one greater in this house than I, and he
has withheld nothing from me except you,
because you are his wife. How then could I
do this great evil and sin against God?' As
she spoke to Joseph day after day, he did
not listen to her to lie beside her or be with
her. Now it happened one day that he went
into the house to do his work, and none of
the men of the household was there inside.
She caught him by his garment, saying, 'Lie
with me!' And he left his garment in her
hand and fled, and went outside. When she
saw that he had left his garment in her hand
and had fled outside, she called to the men
of her household and said to them, 'See,
he has brought in a Hebrew to us to make
sport of us; he came in to me to lie with me,
and I screamed. When he heard that I raised
my voice and screamed, he left his garment
beside me and fled and went outside.'"
(Genesis 39:7-15)

Joseph had a choice to either live his life with integrity and
refuse the advances of Potiphar's wife or succumb to temptation
and dishonor God. We would hope that because Joseph made the
right choice, God would honor his obedience, yet from a human
standpoint, it seems like God abandoned him. When Joseph
refused the advances of this woman, she basically cried "rape" as
he was running from the situation. Joseph did the right thing, yet
here is what happened to him next:

"So she left his garment beside her until his
master came home. Then she spoke to him

**with these words, 'The Hebrew slave, whom
you brought to us, came in to me to make
sport of me; and as I raised my voice and
screamed, he left his garment beside me and
fled outside.' Now when his master heard
the words of his wife, which she spoke to
him, saying, 'This is what your slave did to
me,' his anger burned. So Joseph's master
took him and put him into the jail, the place
where the king's prisoners were confined;
and he was there in the jail." (Genesis 39:16-25)**

Joseph went to jail? For what? Doing what was right?
Running from sin? Honoring God? Honoring his boss? Is that
fair?

What about you? Do you have integrity at work? Do you
refuse to lie or steal? Do you love your spouse regardless of how
he or she treats you? Do you donate your time and money to the
Kingdom of God? What happens when you are doing all the right
things and the bottom falls out? Did Joseph get discouraged about
his situation? Probably. Did he fall apart when his reputation was
challenged? Probably not.

We would assume Joseph had his moments of confusion
and anger, but it seems he never let it affect his trust in God. He
could have become so depressed and discouraged regarding his
circumstances that he shut down and refused to live any more. But
Joseph did not do that. Wherever God placed him, he grew in his
faith and trusted God even more. How about us? Do we become
despondent when things don't go our way? Do we eat more,
drink more, or take more pills to "make it all better?" Do we sleep
more and cocoon ourselves away from the rest of the world?

Joseph had an eternal view of life. The only way a person can
live through an ordeal like Joseph did would be to look at life
through the knowledge that:

God never leaves us.

He has a plan for our lives that sometimes includes pain.

He wants us to learn to wait on Him.

He wants us to learn to trust Him.

Waiting on and trusting God are probably easier said than done, especially when we are in the midst of turmoil; yet because of Joseph's life, we know it can be done. Discouragement comes along when we let our circumstances rule over us. We need to know God has a purpose for everything that comes into our lives. When we believe that another person or a set of circumstances controls our destiny, it makes sense that we would be discouraged when things do not go as we planned.

When we recognize God alone is in charge, even though He seems far away, we can have peace. Joseph who was hated by his brothers, thrown into a well, sold as a slave, and thrown into prison, seemed to embrace his call to wait on the Lord, just like we should. Waiting is difficult, yet during the times when God seems quiet and distant, we have to know in our hearts He continues to work to get us where we need to be.

Once Joseph was in prison, God continued to extend kindness to him:

> **"But the Lord was with Joseph and extended kindness to him, and gave him favor in the sight of the chief jailer. The chief jailer committed to Joseph's charge all the prisoners who were in the jail; so that whatever was done there, he was responsible for it. The chief jailer did not supervise anything under Joseph's charge because the Lord was with him; and whatever he did, the Lord made to prosper." (Genesis 39:21-23)**

Here is the key: God did not remove the bad things in Joseph's life right away. He left Joseph in prison, and not just for a few days but for a few years! Have you ever wondered why God doesn't remove bad things from your life right away? We wonder things like, "Why won't this sickness go away? Why can't I get a job? Why does my marriage keep getting worse instead of better? Why won't my wayward child come home after years and years of being gone?"

Was God mad at Joseph? Did Joseph do something to offend God enough to put him in prison? No! What God was doing was getting Joseph to the exact position where He needed him. For events to unfold as God had planned, Joseph had to be exactly where he was for the time. If we could only remember God sees the entire picture and we can only see what is in front of us, it would change our entire outlook on life. At one point, one of the prisoners he oversaw was being released and Joseph asked him to remember to tell someone in authority that he was there. Joseph assumed he would be getting out as soon, as his friend did, but God had other plans: **"Now it happened at the end of two full years that Pharaoh had a dream, and behold, he was standing by the Nile." (Genesis 41:1)**

Two more years! Just when Joseph thought his life was going to change, God kept him in prison two more years! How frustrated he could have been, wondering what he did wrong and why God was silent, yet we don't read that about Joseph's attitude. God's perfect timing for our lives always prevails. Pharaoh had a dream, and nobody could interpret it until Joseph's long lost friend from prison suddenly remembered him!

> **"'We had a dream on the same night, he and I; each of us dreamed according to the interpretation of his own dream. Now a Hebrew youth was with us there, a servant of the captain of the bodyguard, and we related them to him, and he interpreted our dreams for us. To each one he interpreted according to his own dream. And just as he interpreted for us, so it happened; he restored me**

**in my office, but he hanged him.' Then
Pharaoh sent and called for Joseph, and they
hurriedly brought him out of the dungeon;
and when he had shaved himself and
changed his clothes, he came to Pharaoh."
(Genesis 41:1-11)**

In God's perfect plan there would be a famine, and God knew exactly where Joseph needed to be. He knew that Joseph was the one needed to interpret Pharaoh's dream which would lead to Joseph being second in command and perfectly positioned to help his country during this intense famine. Unfortunately for Joseph, he had to go through a lot of pain and heartache in order for God to get him where he needed to be. Somehow that doesn't seem fair. Wouldn't it be nicer of God to have Joseph show up on vacation and meet Pharaoh on the beach somewhere? Couldn't God just point out Joseph on the beach and let Pharaoh know Joseph would be his man? Wouldn't that have made Joseph's life less difficult?

As we see all through the Bible, God uses trials and tribulation to help us grow. He uses difficult situations to teach us to love and forgive. He uses difficult situations to teach us to be patient and merciful. We would never learn these things if we were sitting on the beach somewhere with no problems! Joseph learned about being unjustly accused. He learned about forgiving his brothers who hurt him so deeply. He learned to lean on God alone and trust Him wherever God took him. Those are lessons that can only be learned through the difficult times in life.

After Joseph became second in command to Pharaoh and the famine became severe, Joseph's brothers showed up to buy grain. Through a series of many events, Joseph finally told his brothers who he was, and after years of heartache, prison, and betrayal, here are Joseph's words to his brothers: **"As for you, you meant evil against me, but God meant it for good in order to bring about this present result, to preserve many people alive."
(Genesis 50:20)**

As we deal with discouragement, we must remember Joseph and his life. We must remember God has a bigger plan that, most of the time, we cannot see. Just as Joseph spent years in prison with no idea what God was doing, many times we go through difficulties and do not understand how God's hand could possibly be in them. But rest on this fact: He is working all things together for a purpose beyond anything we could ever imagine.

Our prayer for this chapter is that you will begin to see that you do not have to be discouraged when life throws you a curve. God has not abandoned you just like He never abandoned Joseph. He had a plan in Genesis, and He has a plan for your life today. It may feel painful and frightening at the time, but think back on the pain and confusion that Joseph must have felt. Memorize **Genesis 50:20.**

> **"But as for you, you meant evil against me; but God meant it for good, in order to bring it about as it is this day, to preserve many people alive."**

Whatever God is allowing in your life that might even seem evil or wrong, God will use it for good. It may take months or years. It may get worse before it gets better. But God has a plan, and you can lay your head on your pillow at night knowing, by faith, that God is working behind the scenes. If you are His child, He has not forgotten you, and He will use whatever has come into your life for good. That, you can count on.

# CHAPTER 4

## *David*
## *Discouragement After Sin*

What is the first thing that comes to your mind when you hear the names of David and Bathsheba? Adultery? Murder? Death? Lying? Have you ever thought about the consequences that come from sin? Have you experienced the heartache and devastation sin produces, not only for the people who commit them but also for those around them? Children are caught in ugly divorces. Spouses are wounded deeply over adulterous affairs. Parents are without children who end up in prison for murder. Children have children because of sex outside of marriage. It all begins with sin, which always leads to consequences, which always leads to discouragement - especially for a Christian.

Do Christians sin? Absolutely. Do Christians feel the effects of sin? Absolutely. How does God deal with a Christian, just like David, who walks away from God's laws and does something against what God asks of him? Does that mean he is not a Christian? Will God ever forgive him? Will he ever have his life back like it was before? What can we do when the pain of sin and a cloud of discouragement hang over our lives?

King David in the Old Testament is a great example of God's grace and mercy. He is also a shining example of how devastating disobedience to God is and why we should stay as far away from sin as possible. God called David a "man after His own heart," so we would assume that if David cared that much for the things of God, he would never disappoint Him. However, God wants us to recognize that we are all human, and even godly people can get themselves into trouble.

Does that give us an excuse to sin or allow us to dishonor God? The Bible uses David's story, *not* to give us an excuse to sin, but to show us how much we hurt ourselves when we do. The pain, anguish, devastation, and the consequences of this choice in David's life prove nothing was worth the short amount of pleasure he got from his encounter with Bathsheba. David never excused his sin, but rather, wanted us to know what it felt like to walk away from the security of God's protective hand and live under the weight of God's heavy hand.

When we first meet David, he is just a boy taking care of his father's sheep. What he doesn't know is his life is about to dramatically change. God has big plans for David. Saul was the King of Israel at the time, but he disregarded God. God told Samuel to anoint a new king that He alone had selected. As Samuel went to the house of Jesse, he found seven brothers who were paraded in front of him. Even though they all looked the part none of them were the chosen one. God told Samuel He looks at the heart, not outward appearances.

> **"Now the Lord said to Samuel, 'How long will you grieve over Saul, since I have rejected him from being king over Israel? Fill your horn with oil and go; I will send you to Jesse the Bethlehemite, for I have selected a king for Myself among his sons.' But Samuel said, 'How can I go? When Saul hears of it, he will kill me.' And the Lord said, 'Take a heifer with you and say, 'I have come to sacrifice to the Lord.' You shall invite Jesse to the sacrifice, and I will**

show you what you shall do; and you shall
anoint for Me the one whom I designate
to you.' So Samuel did what the Lord said,
and came to Bethlehem. And the elders of
the city came trembling to meet him and
said, 'Do you come in peace?' He said, 'In
peace; I have come to sacrifice to the Lord.
Consecrate yourselves and come with me to
the sacrifice.' He also consecrated Jesse and
his sons and invited them to the sacrifice.
When they entered, he looked at Eliab and
thought, 'Surely the Lord's anointed is before
Him.' But the Lord said to Samuel, 'Do not
look at his appearance or at the height of
his stature, because I have rejected him; for
God sees not as man sees, for man looks at
the outward appearance, but the Lord looks
at the heart.' Then Jesse called Abinadab and
made him pass before Samuel. And he said,
'The Lord has not chosen this one either.'
Next Jesse made Shammah pass by. And
he said, 'The Lord has not chosen this one
either.' Thus Jesse made seven of his sons
pass before Samuel. But Samuel said to Jesse,
'The Lord has not chosen these.' And Samuel
said to Jesse, 'Are these all the children?' And
he said, 'There remains yet the youngest,
and behold, he is tending the sheep.' Then
Samuel said to Jesse, 'Send and bring him;
for we will not sit down until he comes here.'
So he sent and brought him in. Now he was
ruddy, with beautiful eyes and a handsome
appearance. And the Lord said, 'Arise, anoint
him; for this is he.' Then Samuel took the
horn of oil and anointed him in the midst of
his brothers; and the Spirit of the Lord came
mightily upon David from that day forward.
And Samuel arose and went to Ramah."
(1 Samuel 16:1-13)

After looking at all the boys, Samuel realized none of them were God's choice for king. When Samuel asked if there were any more children, Jesse said his youngest son was taking care of the sheep. Imagine the scene: all the older brothers who were strong and mature were not God's choice. Instead, God chose the youngest son who was out in the fields taking care of the family's sheep. What was God's choice based on? The heart. David cared about integrity and working hard for his family. He took pride in making sure his flock stayed alive and was well cared for. God could see something in David that his own father couldn't see!

David seemed to have loved God even as a young man. The next time we see David, he is checking on his brothers as they are fighting the dreaded Philistines. Goliath was taunting the army of Israel, and instead of trusting God to fight the battle, the Israelites were running in fear. David showed up and was stunned these men were afraid of Goliath. Sure, he was bigger and scarier than most men, but David looked beyond what he saw to the bottom line: God is stronger than anyone or anything. Instead of running away from Goliath, David ran to him. **1 Samuel 17:26** says, **"Then David spoke to the men who were standing by him, saying, 'What will be done for the man who kills this Philistine and takes away the reproach from Israel? For who is this uncircumcised Philistine, that he should taunt the armies of the living God?'"**

David explained to Saul that God had protected and delivered him from danger when he was watching his father's sheep. Even as a young boy, David trusted God to take care of him. It didn't matter who the enemy was, whether it was a lion or a bear, David gave all the credit to whom credit was due: God alone. Even from an early age, David had a love and trust for God who protected him in the fields.

> **"But David said to Saul, 'Your servant was tending his father's sheep. When a lion or a bear came and took a lamb from the flock, I went out after him and attacked him, and**

rescued it from his mouth; and when he rose
up against me, I seized him by his beard and
struck him and killed him. Your servant has
killed both the lion and the bear; and this
uncircumcised Philistine will be like one of
them, since he has taunted the armies of the
living God.' And David said, 'The Lord who
delivered me from the paw of the lion and
from the paw of the bear, He will deliver
me from the hand of this Philistine.' And
Saul said to David, 'Go, and may the Lord be
with you.'" (1 Samuel 17:34-37)**

After David killed Goliath and he became a household
name, King Saul became jealous of David and tried to kill
him every chance he got. David was on the run from a crazy
king, yet his faith in God to protect him never wavered.
He questioned God, and he confronted God, but he always
trusted Him. That is what God saw in David: his heart.
Through a series of events over many years, David finally
became the King of Israel and because of His love for David,
God blessed him. David loved God and was devoted to Him
until one day when he should have been with his men on the
battlefield he stayed home and his integrity was compromised.
The man after God's own heart now became a man after his
own sinful, lustful heart, and it affected David's life forever.
**"Then it happened in the spring, at the time when
kings go out to battle, that David sent Joab and his
servants with him and all Israel, and they destroyed
the sons of Ammon and besieged Rabbah. But David
stayed at Jerusalem." (2 Samuel 11:1)**

The first problem David encountered was because he was
somewhere he shouldn't have been. He should have been in
the battle, but instead he stayed home. Isn't that how most sin
happens? Maybe it was staying after work with someone you
shouldn't have been with. Maybe it started as an innocent business
lunch. Maybe it began on the internet where you were confronted

with images you could not get out of your mind. However it began, it happened because you were in the wrong place, just like David. Once an idea gets in our heads, we always have a choice. David made the wrong one.

> **"Now when evening came David arose from his bed and walked around on the roof of the king's house, and from the roof he saw a woman bathing; and the woman was very beautiful in appearance. So David sent and inquired about the woman. And one said, 'Is this not Bathsheba, the daughter of Eliam, the wife of Uriah the Hittite?'"**
> **(2 Samuel 11:2-5)**

Remember, God called David a "man after His own heart." That is why this story is so difficult to grasp. How can we love God with all our hearts, yet walk away from Him like David did? How did David devote his life to God yet in one moment see a beautiful woman bathing and, instead of looking the other way, decide to inquire about her? How could a person be devoted to God and fall headlong into sin so quickly?

When David's men brought back the information on Bathsheba to David, they made sure he knew what he was getting into. She was a *daughter* and a *wife*. She was *married*; she was another man's possession. Whoever told David this information was a great friend; they were desperate to make sure David knew exactly why this woman would be off limits, even to the King. Unfortunately, David refused to listen. Perhaps he decided he was bored with his life and needed some new excitement in it. Whatever his rationale, he made a devastating choice. Instead of walking away, he had his messengers bring Bathsheba to sleep with him. **"David sent messengers and took her, and when she came to him, he lay with her; and when she had purified herself from her uncleanness, she returned to her house."** (2 Samuel 11:4)

Please remember one thing: sin always brings consequences:
**"The woman conceived; and she sent and told David, and
said, 'I am pregnant.'" (2 Samuel 11:5)** As Christians, we have
a choice to sin or walk away. If, in fact, we decide to continue
sinning, God promises to always discipline us. Just as we discipline
our own children because we love them, God does the same
with us. Our children reflect us the same way that we, as children
of God, reflect Him. People look at us to see if our faith is real
and if we are truly devoted followers of Christ. When we walk
a disobedient path and others see what we are doing, all along
claiming to be Christians, nothing could hurt the cause of Christ
more.

Deuteronomy 8:5
**"Thus you are to know in your heart that
the Lord your God was disciplining you just
as a man disciplines his son."**

Deuteronomy 11:2
**"Know this day that I am not speaking with
your sons who have not known and who
have not seen the discipline of the Lord your
God—His greatness, His mighty hand and
His outstretched arm."**

Job 5:17
**"Behold, how happy is the man whom God
reproves, so do not despise the discipline of
the Almighty."**

Proverbs 3:11-12
**"My son, do not reject the discipline of the
Lord or loathe His reproof. For whom the
Lord loves He reproves, even as a father
corrects the son in whom he delights."**

Proverbs 6:23
**"For the commandment is a lamp and the**

teaching is light; And reproofs for discipline are the way of life."

**Hebrews 12:5-7**
"And you have forgotten the exhortation which is addressed to you as sons, 'My son, do not regard lightly the discipline of the Lord, Nor faint when you are reproved by Him; For those whom the Lord loves He disciplines, And He scourges every son whom He receives.' It is for discipline that you endure; God deals with you as with sons; for what son is there whom his father does not discipline?"

Once sin is conceived, life becomes a downward spiral. Something that seemed so fun and exciting at the time becomes work. Secrets have to be kept, phone bills have to be hidden, and one lie builds on another. For David, there had to be a cover up. Isn't that always the way it is with sin? We have to lie to protect ourselves. We have to live a life of dishonesty. We lose our integrity and our character. We begin to lose who we are and become someone we were never meant to be. For David, it was not only lying; he turned to murder. Isn't that hard to imagine? The man whom God had protected, trusted so much to live for Him, and given the throne of Israel to, turned his back on God.

We aren't so different than David. This duplicity happens more than we would care to know. Churches are filled with people having adulterous affairs. Schools are filled with Christians walking away from their faith to have sex before marriage. Christians are staying up late at night watching things that are not fitting for a child of God to watch.

As David fell deeper and deeper into this deception, he finally got caught. Most people think they can get away with sin, but the Bible says if you are truly a Christian, God will never let you get away with your sin. It is not in His nature to allow something so destructive to destroy His children, so He uses discipline to get us back on track. Once David made sure Bathsheba's husband was dead, (because David ordered it to happen) he brought her into his house, and she became his wife. Sound like a happy ending? David gets the beautiful girl, and they are going to have a baby together. What could be more exciting for the two of them?

**"Now when the wife of Uriah heard that Uriah her husband was dead, she mourned for her husband. When the time of mourning was over, David sent and brought her to his house and she became his wife; then she bore him a son. But the thing that David had done was evil in the sight of the Lord." (2 Samuel 11:26)**

God does not take our sin lightly. Imagine the people in David's circle who saw what was happening. Imagine what they talked about when he was not around. We can hear it now: "I thought David loved God. I thought David was a moral man. I thought David would always honor God." Instead of promoting fellowship with God and helping draw others to Him, David was destroying his witness, and people were undoubtedly walking away from God after seeing what he had done. That is why it is so important to keep our lives unbound by sin. How it hurts the cause of Christ is beyond our comprehension.

Remember this: there are always consequences. What David did was evil in the sight of the Lord, and even David, or especially David, was the recipient of serious consequences. **2 Samuel 12:1-6** tells us of Nathan, a great friend who confronted David. He did so by telling a story of a poor man and a rich man.

**"Then the Lord sent Nathan to David. And he came to him and said, 'There were two men in one city, the one rich and the other poor. The rich man had a great many flocks and herds. But the poor man had nothing**

except one little ewe lamb which he bought
and nourished; and it grew up together
with him and his children. It would eat of
his bread and drink of his cup and lie in
his bosom, and was like a daughter to him.
Now a traveler came to the rich man, and
he was unwilling to take from his own flock
or his own herd, to prepare for the wayfarer
who had come to him; rather he took the
poor man's ewe lamb and prepared it for the
man who had come to him.' Then David's
anger burned greatly against the man, and
he said to Nathan, 'As the Lord lives, surely
the man who has done this deserves to die.
He must make restitution for the lamb
fourfold, because he did this thing and had
no compassion.'" (2 Samuel 12:1-6)

David somehow missed the point of the story, so
Nathan responded:

"Nathan then said to David, 'You are the
man! Thus says the Lord God of Israel, 'It is
I who anointed you king over Israel and it is
I who delivered you from the hand of Saul. I
also gave you your master's house and your
master's wives into your care, and I gave you
the house of Israel and Judah; and if that had
been too little, I would have added to you
many more things like these!'"
(2 Samuel 12:7-8)

The Lord reminded David everything good that had come
to him in his life was because of God. God chose him to be king
of Israel, God never allowed Saul to kill him, and God gave him
a great life. Not only did He give David everything he needed
and wanted, but He also said He would have given him much
more had he asked! Instead, David turned his back on God. David

forgot the Giver of all his blessings. Isn't that easy to do? God gives us a great job, a wonderful spouse, and beautiful children, yet that doesn't seem enough. Somehow, we become restless, and something tells us the grass is greener on the other side. When the presence of God is not enough for us, we decide to see if we are really missing something in our lives.

Adultery doesn't start at the end. It begins rather innocently with a visual look. Then it gets rationalized into a business lunch and there is talk of unhappiness at home and feelings of misunderstanding. All along this other person is building you up and understanding you more than anyone ever has in your life. That is how it starts. Instead of remembering the commitment you made to God and your spouse and running as far away as possible, you make a second lunch date. It spirals downward from there, just like it did for David.

> **"Why have you despised the word of the Lord by doing evil in His sight? You have struck down Uriah the Hittite with the sword, have taken his wife to be your wife, and have killed him with the sword of the sons of Ammon. Now therefore, the sword shall never depart from your house, because you have despised Me and have taken the wife of Uriah the Hittite to be your wife." Thus says the Lord, 'Behold, I will raise up evil against you from your own household; I will even take your wives before your eyes and give them to your companion, and he will lie with your wives in broad daylight. Indeed you did it secretly, but I will do this thing before all Israel, and under the sun.' Then David said to Nathan, 'I have sinned against the Lord." And Nathan said to David, 'The Lord also has taken away your sin; you shall not die. However, because by this deed you have given occasion to the enemies of**

**the Lord to blaspheme, the child also that
is born to you shall surely die.'" (2 Samuel
12:9-14)**

David had lived an incredibly blessed life, and then it all
changed. God said that his baby conceived in sin would die, and
the sword would never depart from David's house. Both things
happened. Although the consequences were lifelong, David had a
repentant heart and acknowledged he had sinned against the Lord,
so God forgave him. How gracious and merciful God is to take
our sins away and make us white as snow. Even David, a man after
God's own heart who fell deeply into sin, can be forgiven and
restored.

If you, like David, walked into a sinful situation and are
now suffering the consequences, please know God specializes in
restoration. Some of the most heartfelt Psalms were written about
God's grace, mercy, and forgiveness. **Psalm 51** was written right
after Nathan confronted David about his sin.

**"Be gracious to me, O God, according
to Your lovingkindness; according to the
greatness of Your compassion blot out my
transgressions." (Psalm 51:1)**

David knew God so well that he boldly asked God to be
gracious to him. He knew from past experience He was filled
with lovingkindness and compassion. He also knew God alone
could blot out his transgression. That is the God we put our faith
and trust in. He knows we are human, and He knows we are
capable of doing really bad things, yet instead of blotting us out,
He blots out what we have done!

**"Wash me thoroughly from my iniquity
and cleanse me from my sin. For I know
my transgressions, and my sin is ever before
me. Against You, You only, I have sinned and
done what is evil in Your sight, so that You**

**are justified when You speak and blameless when You judge." (Psalm 51:2-4)**

The admirable thing about David was he refused to play the "blame game." He never once said the situation was Bathsheba's fault, that she shouldn't have been bathing where he could see her. He never said her bathing practices were a deliberate way to get inside the palace. He never addressed Bathsheba's sin; he only addressed his own. David had a truly repentant heart, which is exactly what God is after. He begged God to wash him and cleanse him from what he did. It's just like washing and cleansing dirt from our hands. When we are done, the grime has gone down the drain, never to be put back on us again. David knew God could do that but recognized also his sin was always before him. He did not sin with Bathsheba and then casually walk away. David recognized that as much as he was paying the consequences for what he had done, his sin was against God first and foremost.

**"Behold, I was brought forth in iniquity, and in sin my mother conceived me. Behold, You desire truth in the innermost being, And in the hidden part You will make me know wisdom. Purify me with hyssop, and I shall be clean; Wash me, and I shall be whiter than snow. Make me to hear joy and gladness, Let the bones which You have broken rejoice. Hide Your face from my sins And blot out all my iniquities." (Psalm 51:5-9)**

David understood he was human and therefore became a sinner at conception. He recognized God does not want half-hearted obedience; He wants obedience from the innermost part of us. He does not want morality for the sake of morality; instead, He wants us changed from the inside. David also recognized where change would come from: God alone. God is the One who gives us wisdom. God is the One who purifies us and washes our iniquities away. Despite the stain of his sin, David knew God could make him whiter than snow. David wanted joy and peace back in his life, and he knew God is the giver of that gift. All through Psalm 51, David returned to the "man after God's own heart." He recognized what he done, that God was the One offended, and the God he had always trusted could be trusted even with his sin.

> **"Create in me a clean heart, O God, and renew a steadfast spirit within me. Do not cast me away from Your presence And do not take Your Holy Spirit from me. Restore to me the joy of Your salvation And sustain me with a willing spirit." (Psalm 51:10-12)**

If you are feeling discouraged because of something you have done in your past, please know God can take those feelings of guilt and sorrow away and replace them with joy. David recognized he had a heart problem: it had become dirty, and God was the only One who could clean it. David also asked for a renewed, steadfast spirit within himself. Sin can bring such discouragement that the thought of walking away from our faith seems easier than persevering. It seems easier to give up than to stay committed to our relationship with God. When discouragement attacks our lives, we feel so far away from God. His presence seems vague and distant, and the Holy Spirit who comforts us seems to have gone on vacation. God alone is the One who restores our joy to us, and He is the One who gives us a willing spirit to move forward. We just need to ask.

> **"Then I will teach transgressors Your ways, And sinners will be converted to You. Deliver me from bloodguiltiness, O God, the God of my salvation; then my tongue will joyfully sing of Your righteousness. O Lord, open my lips, that my mouth may declare Your praise." (Psalm 51:13-15)**

Because of the forgiveness offered to him, David wanted to teach others they too could be recipients of God's grace and mercy. David wanted others to know that if we fall into a ditch, we don't have to stay there—God alone can pull us out. David wanted others to be assured when true repentance happens, there can be singing, worshipping and praising again.

> **"For You do not delight in sacrifice, otherwise I would give it; You are not pleased with burnt offering. The sacrifices of God are a broken spirit; a broken and a contrite heart, O God, You will not despise. By Your favor do good to Zion; Build the walls of Jerusalem. Then You will delight in righteous sacrifices, In burnt offering and whole burnt offering; Then young bulls will be offered on Your altar." (Psalm 51:16-19)**

The last thing David wanted us to grasp is that God does not delight in our church attendance, our money, or our work in the nursery. He wants a broken spirit and a contrite heart. He wants us to recognize our sin and the devastation it has brought to the heart of God. Only then can God turn our lives around. He does not want flippant confessions over sin. He wants true, heartfelt acknowledgment of how sin affects us and those around us. Then and only then will He restore the joy of our salvation and give us all we need to continue.

Always recognize that God can use our sin to help others. Who can best help someone who is about to have an affair? Someone who has been through the devastation of one. Who can best help someone who is about to have sex outside of marriage? Someone who has been deeply hurt in the same situation. Who can best help someone who is addicted to pornography? Someone who has lost a marriage and a family over this addiction. Use your past to help others avoid the same mistakes by being available and honest. Like David, you can help others through the seasons of discouragement brought on by sin and what is left in its wake. Instead of becoming a victim of discouragement, use it to help others. Because of David's honesty, we have some of the greatest words ever written in the Bible. His life was a testimony to the fact God can and will forgive anything. Paul addressed the idea of helping others in this passage:

> **"Blessed be the God and Father of our
> Lord Jesus Christ, the Father of mercies and
> God of all comfort, who comforts us in
> all our affliction so that we will be able to
> comfort those who are in any affliction with
> the comfort with which we ourselves are
> comforted by God. For just as the sufferings
> of Christ are ours in abundance, so also our
> comfort is abundant through Christ. But
> if we are afflicted, it is for your comfort
> and salvation; or if we are comforted, it is
> for your comfort, which is effective in the
> patient enduring of the same sufferings
> which we also suffer; and our hope for you
> is firmly grounded, knowing that as you
> are sharers of our sufferings, so also you are
> sharers of our comfort." (2 Corinthians 1:3-7)**

David experienced God's mercy, and we can too when we are faced with discouragement over sin. God comforted David and restored his joy. God gave David the perseverance to continue in his faith. Always remember this: God forgives, God restores, and God never stops loving us, even though there will always be consequences for sin. We will need to persevere through the discipline that God puts into our lives, knowing as we feel the sting of God's heavy hand on us, it is because He loves and disciplines us for our own good.

One night, we were watching a television show about a girl who helped steal $3 million from an armored vehicle in Las Vegas. She was on the run for years and years, her family assuming the man she was with had murdered her. Instead, she was living in a foreign country with her abusive boyfriend who helped pull off this heist. She ended up getting pregnant but could not stand to live in the situation with this man, so she took her baby and went into hiding. When her son was 10 years old, she told him she needed to go back to the United States and face whatever consequences her sin had caused. She was looking at 30 years behind bars as she left her son and turned herself in.

When asked why she did this, she said she might have been free on the outside, but inside she was in a prison. She knew if she turned herself in, she would be free from the inner prison that tormented her on a daily basis. She grasped one thing just like David did: sin is exhausting. Just like this woman turned herself in and confessed, so must we do the same. There were serious consequences for her: she is spending five years in prison for what she did. She won't be able to live with her son until he is 15. She has lost her freedom. But in reality, only now is she truly free. Only when we confess what we have done and endure the consequences can we be free.

If you are discouraged over something you have done in your past, confess it, deal with it, and then move on, knowing you are forgiven and can use your past to help others. We have a friend who was sexually abused as a child and became increasingly promiscuous all through her teenage years. She got married young, had affairs, had abortions, and got divorced. But now, she is married to a wonderful man, has beautiful children, and is the most incredible, shining example of God's grace and mercy. She has a ministry that helps those just like her who were molested at a young age. She uses her past to further God's kingdom by helping others move on in their lives.

She understands, just like David did, that sinful living brings pain and consequences, and just like David, she understands the restoration and love of a Savior who has paid the penalty for our sins long ago. God wants from us a broken and contrite heart, and only then can He begin the process to restore and use us. Do not let discouragement get the best of you. The truth we can learn from David' life is that you can let God use your past to help others, and move on to a life of freedom that God alone can give you!

**Psalm 41:4**

"As for me, I said, 'O Lord, be gracious to me; heal my soul, for I have sinned against You.'"

**Psalm 86:15**

"But You, O Lord, are a God merciful and gracious, slow to anger and abundant in lovingkindness and truth."

**Psalm 119:156**

"Great are Your mercies, O Lord; revive me according to Your ordinances."

# CHAPTER 5

## *Jehoshaphat*
## *Discouragement When Fearful*

Coming home from a trip to Europe one summer, we were hit with the usual "jet lag" everyone gets from traveling across different time zones. We had been on an incredible family vacation for a couple weeks which allowed for us to forget all about our businesses back home. We had one particular situation in a business we were glad to forget about for awhile, but once we were back on American soil we realized it was time to "get back to reality!" I (Lisa) am not a worrier by nature; I tend to know God is in control, so I usually don't expend a lot of mental energy worrying about things.

At 3 a.m. after being home one day, I woke up, my body still thinking we were in Europe, and I started to panic about the decisions Rob was going to have to make. Do we keep this particular business going? Do we continue to put more money in it? Do we cut our losses and lose money? Is it worth all the stress? What if our money runs out? What about the employees? What about our family members who were being paid by this business? What would happen to them? Where would they go to work? What if…what if…what if…what if…? Isn't it amazing how fearful we can become so quickly? Isn't it amazing how our minds don't seem to shut off when there is a problem?

I decided to get up and read my Bible. It was quiet in the house as I opened my Bible to where I had been reading in **2 Chronicles 20**. It was one of those moments in my life where the words of God jumped off the pages at me and gave me all the comfort I needed. I realized once again why it is so important to read God's Word on a daily basis. It is always amazing that in God's sovereignty He knows just what we need to get us through any situation. Here is what I read:

> **"Now it came about after this that the sons of Moab and the sons of Ammon, together with some of the Meunites, came to make war against Jehoshaphat. Then some came and reported to Jehoshaphat, saying, 'A great multitude is coming against you from beyond the sea, out of Aram and behold, they are in Hazazon-tamar (that is Engedi).' Jehoshaphat was afraid and turned his attention to seek the Lord, and proclaimed a fast throughout all Judah." (2 Chronicles 20:1-3)**

Jehoshaphat was the King of Judah, and it was reported to him that a great army was coming against him. I was shocked at his response in verse 3: *Jehoshaphat was afraid.* I thought to myself, how comforting it is to know people in the Bible were also afraid! What about you? What do you feel is so threatening in your life that you have become afraid? Finances? Wayward children? Divorce? Loss of job? Health issues? For Jehoshaphat, it was a fear of an attack from a "great multitude," which meant his country was in grave danger. Imagine his "what if" thoughts: What if they kill my family? What if we are kidnapped and taken to a foreign country? What will happen to our homes? What will happen to our neighbors? What if we are not strong enough to fight this battle? What if, what if, what if…? Don't we spend an enormous amount of time on the "what ifs" in our lives? How many of these things actually come to pass?

Then I read what Jehoshaphat did. Instead of worrying, he "turned his attention to seek the Lord and he proclaimed a fast." His first reaction was fear, and then his fear turned to the Lord! Think how much wasted energy we use when we worry! What Jehoshaphat recognized was that God was in control, and he wanted to make sure he called on the One who could stop this army from coming upon his tiny nation.

Jehoshaphat evidently knew God and had a close relationship with Him. As we read and study our Bibles, we become knowledgeable about the true character of the God of the Bible, not some god we invent in our heads. How many times have we heard people say things like "my god would never do that!" Exactly our point: the true God of the Bible is completely different from the gods we make up. Think about these sayings:

My God would never send anyone to hell.
My God would never kill women and children in the Old Testament.
My God would never allow my child to die.
My God would never allow me to get cancer.
My God would never want me to be unhappy.
My God does not control hurricanes, tornadoes, and wild fires.
My God would never let my spouse walk out on me.
My God would never allow my child to go to prison.

The problem with our society is that many people make up what they think God should and shouldn't do. They have preconceived ideas that God is only here to make them happy, healthy, and wealthy. But here is what the true God of the Bible is really like:

My God does send people to hell if they do not place their faith in Jesus alone.
My God did kill women and children in the Old Testament as judgment for sin.
My God does allow children to die for His own purposes.

My God does allow very godly men and women to
    get cancer.

My God cares much more for my holiness than
    my happiness.

My God does control natural disasters and uses them to bring
    others to Himself.

My God does allow your spouse to walk out so you can
    "comfort others."

My God does allow people to go to prison because that is
    where many find Him.

We have to recognize that God's ways are never like our ways. **Isaiah 55:9** says, **"For as the heavens are higher than the earth, so are My ways higher than your ways and My thoughts than your thoughts."** In order to grow in our relationship with God, we have to recognize He thinks differently than we do. His thoughts are different from ours. What we think of as a tragedy, He uses to bring others to Himself. What we consider fearful, He uses so we will learn to trust Him. We need to learn to align ourselves with what He wants in our lives, not what we want in our lives. We are a nation filled with people wanting our own way. We are a Church filled with people wanting our own way. We are families filled with people wanting our own way. Yet God is calling us to look at our lives through His eyes and to walk in His path.

We need to start recognizing that God holds our life, our breath, and all our ways in His hands. We tend to think our lives are our own, so when something tragic or frightening comes along, we think God has forgotten us, or maybe He is mad at us. We have to realize we are His, and He wants to use us to bring others to Himself. Sometimes that means heartache, yet as we learn to trust Him more and more, the "things" of our lives start meaning less and less.

> **"Now, Israel, what does the Lord your God require from you, but to fear the Lord your God, to walk in all His ways and love Him,**

and to serve the Lord your God with all your
heart and with all your soul." (Deuteronomy
10:12)

God requires us to fear Him (or revere Him), walk in His
ways (not our own ways), love Him (not love ourselves more), and
serve Him (not serve ourselves). He wants a total devotion to Him
with *all* our heart and *all* our soul. He doesn't want us to partially
love and serve Him—He wants *all* of us. When we begin to grasp
that our lives are His, then we will move away from fear because
we can trust that whatever comes in our lives is always filtered
through His loving hands.

**2 Samuel 22:31** says, **"As for God, His way is blameless;
the word of the Lord is tested; He is a shield to all who
take refuge in Him."** When we begin to be fearful of things
that come in our lives, we have to learn to take refuge in Him, not
our family, friends, bank accounts, or jobs. He wants us to place
our trust in our relationship with Him, not our relationships with
others. He alone is where we need to go for the comfort we need.
He promises to be our shield and protector.

**Psalm 37:34** reads, **"Wait for the Lord and keep His way,
and He will exalt you to inherit the land; when the wicked
are cut off, you will see it."** A large part of trusting God with
all our situations is learning to wait for Him to move. This has
been the hardest part for us! We live in a "microwave" society
where we want things now. If we want popcorn, we don't want
to put oil and kernels in a pan and wait until it heats up and pops.
That might take 15 minutes! We want our popcorn in 2 minutes
with no mess to clean up! The same rings true in our Christian
lives. We want the deal to go through now. We want our children
to love the Lord with all their hearts now. We want our wayward
child to come home now. Yet most times, God is taking His time
so we will learn to trust Him! If He gave us everything we wanted
right now, would we spend time praying? If everything always
went our way, would we ever acknowledge our need for God?
Probably not! We have to learn that His timing is always perfect,

even though He seems to always wait until the very last minute!

Our son played football for Wheaton College, and in one particular game they were playing one of their rival schools. The game went back and forth for four quarters, and it came down to a score of 28-24. Wheaton was winning, but the other team had the ball. It was 4th down and goal—a touchdown was only 6 yards and 37 seconds away for the other team, and our son Jesse sacked the quarterback for a Wheaton win! It was a dramatic ending to a very suspenseful game, and we thought how much that was like God! Most times He waits for 4th and goal with 37 seconds left in our lives as He continues to teach us to trust Him until He sacks our problem — which usually is at the end of the game!

In your life, it could be you are facing the dissolution of your marriage or the strain of a financial crisis. Maybe your child is a drug addict, and one more episode will put him in jail. And then God steps in and redeems your marriage, an unexpected check comes in the mail, or God saves your child. Regardless of the circumstances, He wants us to trust Him with our problems all along. That is the incredible God that we place our hope and trust in.

As we look back to **2 Chronicles 20:4-11**, this is how Jehoshaphat handled his fear:

> **"So Judah gathered together to seek help from the Lord; they even came from all the cities of Judah to seek the Lord. Then Jehoshaphat stood in the assembly of Judah and Jerusalem, in the house of the Lord before the new court, and he said, 'O Lord, the God of our fathers, are You not God in the heavens? And are You not ruler over all the kingdoms of the nations? Power and might are in Your hand so that no one can stand against You. Did You not, O our God, drive out the inhabitants of this land**

**before Your people Israel and give it to the descendants of Abraham Your friend forever? They have lived in it, and have built You a sanctuary there for Your name, saying, 'Should evil come upon us, the sword, or judgment, or pestilence, or famine, we will stand before this house and before You (for Your name is in this house) and cry to You in our distress, and You will hear and deliver us.' Now behold, the sons of Ammon and Moab and Mount Seir, whom You did not let Israel invade when they came out of the land of Egypt (they turned aside from them and did not destroy them), see how they are rewarding us by coming to drive us out from Your possession which You have given us as an inheritance.'"**

Instead of focusing on his fears, Jehoshaphat focused on God. He remembered how God had always come through for the Israelites in the past. He focused on who God was and how incredibly powerful He was! Look at what he said to God:

*Are you not the God in the heavens?*
*Are you not the ruler of all the kingdoms and nations?*
*Power and might are in Your hands!*
*No one can stand against You!*
*You drove out the inhabitants of our nation in order to give it to us!*
*We will cry out to You and You will hear us and deliver us!*

Because Jehoshaphat knew God so well and remembered what He had done in the past, he knew he could trust Him! He didn't have to be fearful; instead, he recognized the power and strength God had to solve his problem. He knew the minute the God of the Universe, the ruler of all kingdoms and nations, and the One who had the power and might in His hands got involved, Jehoshaphat's problems were over.

**2 Chronicles 20:12** gives us the answer to any issues we have in our lives. **"O our God, will You not judge them? For we are powerless before this great multitude who are coming against us; nor do we know what to do, but our eyes are on You."**

So the answer is to recognize that we are powerless, and put our eyes on Him alone. How simple that is in words yet how difficult to live out! In **Matthew 14:24-33,** we read that the disciples were in a boat in a storm:

> "But the boat was already a long distance from the land, battered by the waves; for the wind was contrary. And in the fourth watch of the night He came to them, walking on the sea. When the disciples saw Him walking on the sea, they were terrified, and said, 'It is a ghost!' And they cried out in fear. But immediately Jesus spoke to them, saying, 'Take courage, it is I; do not be afraid.' Peter said to Him, 'Lord, if it is You, command me to come to You on the water.' And He said, 'Come!' And Peter got out of the boat, and walked on the water and came toward Jesus. But seeing the wind, he became frightened, and beginning to sink, he cried out, 'Lord, save me!' Immediately Jesus stretched out His hand and took hold of him, and said to him, 'You of little faith, why did you doubt?' When they got into the boat, the wind stopped. And those who were in the boat worshipped Him, saying, 'You are certainly God's Son!'"

Peter learned a valuable lesson: things fall apart when we take our eyes off of Jesus! We have to look to Him through the storms. We have to look to Him when our world seems to be falling apart. We have to keep our eyes on Him when tragedy strikes. If we don't, we will sink. We will sink into depression, self pity, anger, and hurt. We will become bitter and sad. We will let unforgiveness take control of our lives. Peter learned that Jesus would have kept him from sinking in the storm if he had kept his eye on Him. The minute he started looking at the waves and the wind, was the minute he started to sink.

When this little lesson was over for Peter, Jesus calmed the storm. Here is an interesting thought: if there had not been a storm, would Peter have ever learned who Jesus was? If this event had never happened, would Peter have grown in his relationship with Christ? Can you see why God allows trials, tragedies, and hurts come into our lives? God wants us to look to Him as the only One who can calm the storms. Unfortunately, we live in a society where we are sure we can handle any problem. If we are sick, we can find the best doctor. If we are out of a job, we rely on our great resumés. If we need medicine, we trust in our insurance company. If our spouse is walking out on us, we can purchase a new car or a new house to make him or her happy enough to stay. We end up trusting in our ability to do something instead of trusting in God's ability.

Visiting poor countries has shown us a lot about what truly trusting God really means. We met a woman who had cancer, and there was no medicine for her. She could only pray and trust God, and He healed her. When there is no medicine, insurance, or money, they pray, and God provides. The only thing they know how to do is keep their eyes on Him because He is the only source for what they need. For people who understand this concept, trusting Jesus is their first option. For those of us who trust in ourselves, trusting in Jesus is usually our last option.

The last thing Jehoshaphat did was recognize this, **"Listen, all Judah and the inhabitants of Jerusalem and King Jehoshaphat: thus says the Lord to you, 'Do not fear or be dismayed because of this great multitude, for the battle is not yours but God's.'" (2 Chronicles 20:15)** We need never fear because if we are Christians, children of God, the battle is always His. He is molding us and shaping us just like a potter shapes a piece of clay into something beautiful. If the clay were alive, it would probably tell us that being molded isn't too much fun! The same holds true for us. We need to look at every situation in our lives as an opportunity to be molded into what God wants us to look like.

That is why our problems are His problems. The financial battles we are facing, we need to give to Him. The emotional relationship problems we have, we need to give to Him. The medical problems we are facing, we have to give to Him. The day we can envision laying all of these problems at the feet of Jesus and saying "My eyes are on You, this battle is Yours, and I am trusting You to work this out however You want," will be the day we can have peace. If we lose all our money, God will use it for a purpose. If our wayward child doesn't come home for 10 years, God will use it for a purpose. If our sickness gets worse, God will use it for a purpose.

That is what keeping your eyes on Him means. Remember, He is the God of the Universe who flung the stars, the moon, and the sun into the sky. He created the planets and galaxies. Is He not big enough to solve our problems? Can He heal? Can He save your marriage? Can He save your child from self destruction? Can He get you a job? Of course He can — He is GOD! But many times He says, "Wait," because He wants us to get to the point of desperation so that we learn to trust Him — not ourselves, not our bank account, and not our friends or family. He wants us to trust Him alone to solve our problems in the best manner that gives Him the most glory.

Here is how the story of Jehoshaphat ends:

> **"'Tomorrow go down against them. Behold, they will come up by the ascent of Ziz, and you will find them at the end of the valley in front of the wilderness of Jeruel. You need not fight in this battle; station**

yourselves, stand and see the salvation of the
Lord on your behalf, O Judah and Jerusalem.
Do not fear or be dismayed; tomorrow
go out to face them, for the Lord is with
you.' Jehoshaphat bowed his head with his
face to the ground, and all Judah and the
inhabitants of Jerusalem fell down before
the Lord, worshiping the Lord. The Levites,
from the sons of the Kohathites and of the
sons of the Korahites, stood up to praise the
Lord God of Israel, with a very loud voice.
They rose early in the morning and went
out to the wilderness of Tekoa; and when
they went out, Jehoshaphat stood and said,
'Listen to me, O Judah and inhabitants of
Jerusalem, put your trust in the Lord your
God and you will be established. Put your
trust in His prophets and succeed.' When he
had consulted with the people, he appointed
those who sang to the Lord and those who
praised Him in holy attire, as they went out
before the army and said, 'Give thanks to the
Lord, for His lovingkindness is everlasting.'
When they began singing and praising,
the Lord set ambushes against the sons of
Ammon, Moab and Mount Seir, who had
come against Judah; so they were routed.
For the sons of Ammon and Moab rose
up against the inhabitants of Mount Seir
destroying them completely; and when they
had finished with the inhabitants of Seir,
they helped to destroy one another. When
Judah came to the lookout of the wilderness,
they looked toward the multitude, and
behold, they were corpses lying on the
ground, and no one had escaped. When
Jehoshaphat and his people came to take
their spoil, they found much among them,

including goods, garments and valuable
things which they took for themselves,
more than they could carry. And they
were three days taking the spoil because
there was so much. Then on the fourth day
they assembled in the valley of Beracah,
for there they blessed the Lord. Therefore
they have named that place 'The Valley of
Beracah' until today. Every man of Judah
and Jerusalem returned with Jehoshaphat at
their head, returning to Jerusalem with joy,
for the Lord had made them to rejoice over
their enemies. They came to Jerusalem with
harps, lyres and trumpets to the house of the
Lord. And the dread of God was on all the
kingdoms of the lands when they heard that
the Lord had fought against the enemies of
Israel." (2 Chronicles 20:16-29)

After reading this passage the morning we got back from our
trip to Israel, I realized that if my life is in His hands, then He
will determine the outcome of our businesses regardless of my
worrying about it! I could only do the one thing that I had any
ability to do: pray. I could pray for wisdom for Rob and our oldest
son who had to make these decisions. I could pray for God to
turn the hearts of those we were having problems with. I could
pray God would give us the patience to wait and see what He
would do. God used the life of Jehoshaphat in a great way that
morning to show me that fear is debilitating. It causes people to
look within themselves for answers instead of looking to God
for answers. It was comforting to know all of my battles are His
and He has a perfect time for everything to happen. He is always
working behind the scenes, and when we can't see His hand, that
doesn't mean He isn't there. It just gives us a greater opportunity
to "keep our eyes on Him!"

Psalm 25:15

"My eyes are continually toward the Lord,
for He will pluck my feet out of the net."

Psalm 17:8

"Keep me as the apple of the eye; hide me
in the shadow of Your wings...."

Psalm 32:8

"I will instruct you and teach you in the way
which you should go; I will counsel you with
My eye upon you."

Psalm 33:18

"Behold, the eye of the Lord is on those
who fear Him, on those who hope for His
lovingkindness."

Psalm 94:9

"He who planted the ear, does He not hear?
He who formed the eye, does He not see?"

Psalm 145:15

"The eyes of all look to You, and You give
them their food in due time."

# CHAPTER 6

## *Elijah*
## *Discouragement After a Victory*

Sometimes I feel sorry for those who win the Super Bowl. I always try to imagine what their lives must feel like the day or the week after the big win. It has to be the most incredible feeling to have worked so hard to get to the place where they win the most important game of the season. They get the trophy, the ring, the recognition...and then they have to go back to the real world. Now the pressure is on to do it again - work harder, get stronger, and run faster so they don't lose the next year. There has to be some measure of discouragement when it is all over.

Probably you've never won the Super Bowl, but maybe, instead, your goal was the promotion you wanted for so long and now have. What about the wedding you dreamed of your whole life that is now over? What about the dream of children when the last one just left for college? Many times in life, discouragement comes after some sort of victory. It is so easy to get wrapped up in our dreams and desires for our lives, yet when we finally achieve them, there can be a sense of loss. How is it possible to have waited for something so long, gotten it, and then become depressed?

We have heard that the hardest day for a pastor is Monday. Pastors work all week preparing for their sermons. They present them, share with people, pour their lives into the congregation, and then Monday comes. Along with exhaustion comes a sense of discouragement. What does the Bible say to do when these times come into our lives? Thankfully, the Bible gives us a great example in the person of Elijah.

We find Elijah in **1 Kings 17** coming up against the wicked king Ahab. Ahab was the king over Israel, and the Bible says this of him:

> **"Ahab the son of Omri did evil in the sight of the Lord more than all who were before him. It came about, as though it had been a trivial thing for him to walk in the sins of Jeroboam the son of Nebat, that he married Jezebel the daughter of Ethbaal king of the Sidonians, and went to serve Baal and worshiped him. So he erected an altar for Baal in the house of Baal which he built in Samaria. Ahab also made the Asherah. Thus Ahab did more to provoke the Lord God of Israel than all the kings of Israel who were before him." (1 Kings 16:30-33)**

Elijah was a prophet of God who was sent to confront those who worshipped Baal. Baal was a false god who supposedly provided rain necessary for the fertility of the land, and Elijah's confrontation of Baal worshippers included the wicked King Ahab and his wicked wife Jezebel. At this point, Elijah knew he was sent by God, knew he had a purpose, and was more than willing to do what God was calling him to do. He did not seem afraid; instead, he seemed to put his complete trust in God to take care of him, and he didn't seem to have a problem confronting this depraved King. **"Now Elijah the Tishbite, who was of the settlers of Gilead, said to Ahab, 'As the Lord, the God of Israel lives, before whom I stand, surely there shall be neither dew nor rain these years, except by my word.'" (1 Kings 17:1)** As soon as Elijah told Ahab there would be no more rain or dew, God told Elijah to hide.

"The word of the Lord came to him, saying, 'Go away from here and turn eastward, and hide yourself by the brook Cherith, which is east of the Jordan. It shall be that you will drink of the brook, and I have commanded the ravens to provide for you there.' So he went and did according to the word of the Lord, for he went and lived by the brook Cherith, which is east of the Jordan. The ravens brought him bread and meat in the morning and bread and meat in the evening, and he would drink from the brook. It happened after a while that the brook dried up, because there was no rain in the land." (1 Kings 17:2-7)

The key to avoiding discouragement is realizing that things change in life. If we can prepare ourselves, change will not devastate us when it comes. The economy will not always be stable. We may lose our job. We may get sick. We may have to move. That is just part of living life on this earth. The stabilizing factor in our lives has to be the knowledge that God is in control of everything. God stopped the rain, yet He provided Elijah with drink from the brook and food brought by birds! We have to recognize God promises to take care of us, and instead of falling apart when our circumstances change, we have to fall under His umbrella of protection.

Because of the drought, there was no more water, so God sent Elijah to a widow who would provide for him. Times were tough and she also was starving, yet God provided for her in a miraculous way.

"Then Elijah said to her, 'Do not fear; go, do as you have said, but make me a little bread cake from it first and bring it out to me, and afterward you may make one for yourself and for your son.' For thus says the Lord

**God of Israel, 'The bowl of flour shall not be
exhausted, nor shall the jar of oil be empty,
until the day that the Lord sends rain on the
face of the earth.'" (1 Kings 17:13-14)**

Elijah and the widow were recipients of God's amazing care
and provision, which He also promises to us. We have to learn to
recognize that provision may come in the form of an unexpected
check in the mail, a friend who buys you groceries, or a bill that
gets paid anonymously.

There is another side to God providing for our needs:
He might want us to help provide for someone else. Do you
know God may use your financial resources to be the answer
to someone who is crying out to Him in need? We have to be
willing, just like the widow, to help when called upon. Because of
her obedience, God kept food in her cupboards until the drought
was over.

Three years later, Elijah heard from the Lord. We often wonder
what he was thinking during those three years. Maybe he was
wondering, "Where is God? Why isn't He letting me know what
is going on? When will this drought be over? Doesn't He see the
devastation this is bringing? Doesn't He know that people and
animals are dying? Doesn't He care?" Aren't those the questions
we ask when things aren't going the way we think they should?
Don't we question God and His care for us? Left to ourselves,
without the Bible to show us an eternal perspective, we would
always question Him. We have to read His Word so when things
are not going as planned, we can be comforted, knowing He really
is in control. Elijah didn't seem too concerned that he wasn't
hearing from God; he just continued living his life until he heard
from the Lord:

**"Now it happened after many days that the
word of the Lord came to Elijah in the third
year, saying, 'Go, show yourself to Ahab, and
I will send rain on the face of the earth.' So**

Elijah went to show himself to Ahab. Now
the famine was severe in Samaria." (1 Kings
18:1-2)

"When Ahab saw Elijah, Ahab said to him,
'Is this you, you troubler of Israel?' He said,
'I have not troubled Israel, but you and
your father's house have, because you have
forsaken the commandments of the Lord
and you have followed the Baals. Now then
send and gather to me all Israel at Mount
Carmel, together with 450 prophets of Baal
and 400 prophets of the Asherah, who eat
at Jezebel's table.' So Ahab sent a message
among all the sons of Israel and brought the
prophets together at Mount Carmel. Elijah
came near to all the people and said, 'How
long will you hesitate between two opinions?
If the Lord is God, follow Him; but if Baal,
follow him.' But the people did not answer
him a word." (1 Kings 18:17-21)

Elijah was on a mission to prove to the nation of Israel
that there was only one true God. They would need to choose
between God and their false gods. Elijah needed them to see the
error of their ways, so he set up a competition between the false
prophets of Baal and God. He wanted to prove to Israel there is
only one God and they needed to return to Him.

"Then Elijah said to the people, 'I alone
am left a prophet of the Lord, but Baal's
prophets are 450 men. Now let them give
us two oxen; and let them choose one ox
for themselves and cut it up, and place it
on the wood, but put no fire under it; and
I will prepare the other ox and lay it on the
wood, and I will not put a fire under it. Then
you call on the name of your god, and I will

**call on the name of the Lord, and the God
who answers by fire, He is God.' And all the
people said, 'That is a good idea.'" (1 Kings
18:22-24)**

Of course, God won. Baal was silent, and God came through
with fire that consumed the burnt offering and the water in the
ditches. Elijah told the people to seize the false prophets and kill
them all. Then he waited. He prayed and waited for a cloud, and
then prayed and waited some more. After his seventh time praying
for rain, he saw a cloud and knew God would bring the rain.
He then ran full speed ahead of Ahab into Jezreel. Elijah had an
incredible victory, one that had been three years in the making.
During that time, God stopped the rain, provided Elijah with food
and water, won a competition, killed false prophets, and provided
rain. Then with supernatural speed, Elijah ended up back in the
city. That is where the problem began: Elijah fell apart.

Can you imagine seeing all the miracles that Elijah saw? What
if God supernaturally filled your flour canister each day? What
if He stopped the rain just like He told you He would? What if
you saw His power as fire came down from heaven? Wouldn't that
make you feel God was on your side no matter what? Ironically,
exactly the opposite happened to Elijah. He became fearful and
depressed and wanted to die.

**"Now Ahab told Jezebel all that Elijah
had done, and how he had killed all the
prophets with the sword. Then Jezebel sent
a messenger to Elijah, saying, 'So may the
gods do to me and even more, if I do not
make your life as the life of one of them
by tomorrow about this time.' And he was
afraid and arose and ran for his life and
came to Beersheba, which belongs to Judah,
and left his servant there. But he himself
went a day's journey into the wilderness, and
came and sat down under a juniper tree; and**

**he requested for himself that he might die, and said, 'It is enough; now, O Lord, take my life, for I am not better than my fathers.' He lay down and slept under a juniper tree; and behold, there was an angel touching him, and he said to him, 'Arise, eat.'" (1 Kings 19:1-5)**

Elijah experienced first hand the awesome power of God yet he suddenly became afraid of wicked Jezebel. She threatened him, and he ran for his life. Instead of remembering the care and concern God had showered him with, he became hopeless. Afraid and exhausted, he asked to die. How could that happen? How could someone so entrenched in doing God's work become like this? It would be understandable if God never answered a single prayer or never showed up in Elijah's life, but that was not the case. Elijah and God were an unstoppable team, yet somehow, Elijah lost sight of who God was.

That is easy to do in life. I'm sure we have all prayed for things, and God has answered in a favorable manner. I'm sure we have seen God move in the hearts of the unsaved whose lives have been drastically changed by a relationship with Jesus. I would bet we have seen the hand of God in many areas in our lives, yet we have short memories when it comes to what God has done in the past. Just like Elijah, we forget who controls everything on this earth, and when that happens, we no longer look at life with eternal eyes. All we can see is our overwhelming circumstances, which paralyze us with fear.

We think prophets of God must have been so different from us, but as the Bible portrays, they became afraid and overwhelmed with life just like we do. They had the same choice we have as well. Do we continue along the path running away from God, or do we turn back to Him? Elijah was running away, but God wanted Elijah to learn a valuable lesson: that everything depends on Him. Once we come to that realization, we can take the back seat and relax. God has to be the One to come through. He has to give me peace, He has to give me the strength to trust Him. Elijah thought he was in control, and that he had to run away to safety. He forgot God was his protector. When we start feeling afraid and anxious, we have to learn to stop and ask Him to give us what we need for the moment. We can never be filled with lasting peace and joy from our own effort.

Look at this next passage and see how incredible our God is:

> **"[Elijah] lay down and slept under a juniper tree; and behold, there was an angel touching him, and he said to him, 'Arise, eat.' Then he looked and behold, there was at his head a bread cake baked on hot stones, and a jar of water. So he ate and drank and lay down again. The angel of the Lord came again a second time and touched him and said, 'Arise, eat, because the journey is too great for you.' So he arose and ate and drank, and went in the strength of that food forty days and forty nights to Horeb, the mountain of God." (1 Kings 19:5-8)**

God wasn't mad at Elijah; He comforted him. He made sure he had food and water and allowed for a time of rest. This is such a beautiful picture of God's grace. He wants to be there for us, comfort us in our exhaustion, and give us what we need—and what we need can only come from Him.

In Elijah's mind, he was done with everything. He had been through fear, rejection, and anxiety. He was ready to quit the rat race of life, which would be understandable if his life were falling apart. Instead, he felt this way after experiencing some of the most incredible miracles a person could experience. He stood up for his faith against the most wicked, evil king, and he won. Still, depression and discouragement followed. The same could be true for us. We get the job or win the game or see our children get

married, and instead of joy and happiness, we sink into a pit. God
tells us what Elijah did:

> **"Then he came there to a cave and lodged
> there; and behold, the word of the Lord
> came to him, and He said to him, 'What
> are you doing here, Elijah?' He said, 'I have
> been very zealous for the Lord, the God of
> hosts; for the sons of Israel have forsaken
> Your covenant, torn down Your altars and
> killed Your prophets with the sword. And I
> alone am left; and they seek my life, to take
> it away.'" (1 Kings 19:9-10)**

This happens when we begin to look inward instead of
upward. Instead of looking at God and the blessings in our lives,
we begin to spiral into self pity. Isn't it great to know we are not
alone, that the Bible shares with us the lives of other men and
women who faced the same things we do? Elijah starting telling
God all the great things he had done for Him. Haven't we all
been there? I go to church, God; I am honest at work, God; I put
money in the offering plate, God. Why can't I seem to get out of
this pit of darkness? Why am I suddenly fearful and anxious? Why
has Your presence seemed to have disappeared? Even though You
have done so much for me, why am I am still frightened?

Then God came to Elijah with this:

> **"So He said, 'Go forth and stand on the
> mountain before the Lord.' And behold,
> the Lord was passing by! And a great and
> strong wind was rending the mountains and
> breaking in pieces the rocks before the Lord;
> but the Lord was not in the wind. And after
> the wind an earthquake, but the Lord was
> not in the earthquake. After the earthquake
> a fire, but the Lord was not in the fire; and
> after the fire a sound of a gentle blowing.**

**When Elijah heard it, he wrapped his face in his mantle and went out and stood in the entrance of the cave. And behold, a voice came to him and said, 'What are you doing here, Elijah?'" (1 Kings 19:11-13)**

Sometimes it is that still, small voice we need to hear. God is always at work behind the scenes, and as much as we need the thunder and the wind and the earthquake—the big things to happen—most of the time He is working quietly. Elijah had seen incredible things, yet something small like a threat from Jezebel caused him to lose faith and run in fear.

When we have something wonderful happen in our lives, let us remember how easy it is to fall into a deep, dark hole of discouragement and depression as soon as it is over. Somehow in all the excitement, we seem to lose sight of God, and many times we need to feel His gentle touch and His soft voice to know He is still there. Nothing has changed. He is still the God of miracles. He is still the God who controls everything. The problem is with us. However, once we become aware that huge victories can also bring huge discouragements, then we can begin to prepare for them.

The story ends with Elisha, the prophet who took Elijah's place, commissioning three men who would eventually destroy Baal worship in Israel. God is always working in our lives. Sometimes we know it and feel it, and other times we cannot see Him at all. It is at those times that we need to ask Him for that still, small voice to encourage us to keep going. He is the only One who can give us the encouragement we need.

# CHAPTER 7

## *Habakkuk*
## *Feeling the Pain and*
## *Heartache of the World*

Israel and the Palestinians have been at war since the days of Abraham. **Genesis 16:11-12** reads,

> **"The angel of the Lord said to her further, 'Behold, you are with child, and you will bear a son; and you shall call his name Ishmael, because the Lord has given heed to your affliction. He will be a wild donkey of a man, his hand will be against everyone, and everyone's hand will be against him; and he will live to the east of all his brothers.'"**

Abraham had two sons: Isaac and Ishmael. The descendants of Isaac make up the nation of Israel, and the descendants of Ishmael make up the Arab nations. The Bible says this war between them will never end until the Prince of Peace, Jesus, returns. Because of the turmoil between Israel and Arab nations, living side by side is difficult for both groups. Both feel they belong on the land of Israel, both feel their religion is the right one, and the tension cannot be denied.

On our trip to Israel as we came out of Hezekiah's Tunnel, the bus that was supposed to pick us up was waiting for us on top of the hill. It couldn't get through because a taxi cab had been in an accident: it had hit a horse. Because of the accident, we had to walk through a little town which was on the Palestinian side. We saw despair at its worst: crowds of people who were angry because the horse had been hit and children who couldn't escape the hatred and war. One little boy threw a rock at one of the people on our tour bus.

After we got on our bus, I (Lisa) was sitting next to the window, and I saw a little boy with a dirty face looking up at us. I was overwhelmed with sadness, and I started crying. "This isn't fair," I was thinking. This little boy has no chance in life. He was born into a false religion, one that is teaching him hatred for Israel, hatred for Americans, and just plain hatred. He was so sweet and innocent looking, and my heart hurt for the life he had to live. There was garbage everywhere he went. There was war, guns, and bloodshed. I became mad at God for the injustices of the world.

I went back to our room that night with a very heavy heart. I thought how easy it is to live in America where we can go to our Christian churches, have nice clothes, and go to nice restaurants. We don't give a second thought to our garbage collection services and that we don't have to worry about being gunned down by an enemy. We take for granted that when we turn a faucet on we will have hot running water and we can earn money to buy the things we want. It all suddenly seemed so wrong, so unfair. Why, God? What are You thinking? People are suffering, children are dying, and you seem to be nowhere in sight.

What happens when we feel like God has disappeared? What happens when we feel mad at God or we don't understand why the world looks like it does? What happens when the World Trade Center collapses and thousands of people lose loved ones? What happens when you feel like God has abandoned you? What do you do when you cannot seem to get past the unfairness that this world has to offer?

I am thankful that someone taught me the importance of reading my Bible, for without knowing what it had to say, I don't know where I would have turned. Feeling hopeless and without solid ground to stand on is frightening. That night in the hotel room, a book of the Bible came alive to me and allowed me to be comforted. It was then that I realized that most people, without a knowledge of God and His Word, could easily fall apart and walk away from whatever faith they have. Without a strong foundation in God's Word, there is no true comfort in any situation.

I turned in my Bible to the book of Habakkuk and read **Habakkuk 1:1-4**:

> **"The oracle which Habakkuk the prophet
> saw. How long, O Lord, will I call for help,
> and You will not hear? I cry out to You,
> 'Violence!' Yet You do not save. Why do You
> make me see iniquity, and cause me to look
> on wickedness? Yes, destruction and violence
> are before me; strife exists and contention
> arises. Therefore the law is ignored and
> justice is never upheld. For the wicked
> surround the righteous; therefore justice
> comes out perverted."**

There is something in us that longs to tell God how we feel, but we are afraid He will get mad at us. Who am I to tell God He is doing things wrong? Who am I to tell God He seems unfair? Who am I to tell God I feel angry with Him? Most of us are afraid we might be struck by lightning if we are honest with God! But it is comforting to know that the prophets of God told Him exactly how they felt. Habakkuk basically told God that for as long as he had been calling out to Him he questioned whether God was even listening! He accused God of not saving people and allowing destruction and violence. He even accused God because the wicked were winning!

Have you ever felt that way? Have you ever wondered why

wicked people who have no love for God seem to get ahead in life? Have you ever wondered why the poor who love Jesus seem to have problems and sadness in their lives? Aren't Christians supposed to be taken care of better than the wicked? I wondered the same thing, and that was when I realized how gracious God is because He allows us in our humanness to ask questions. Most often, we never get the answers we want. Instead, we have to learn to trust in His ability to run this world however He sees fit. However in the case of Habakkuk, God did answer: **"Look among the nations! Observe! Be astonished! Wonder! Because I am doing something in your days— you would not believe if you were told." (Habakkuk 1:5)**

I love this answer because God is always working behind the scenes, and we rarely understand what is going on at the time. God told Habakkuk that even if He told him what He was doing, Habakkuk would not believe it! The same is true for us. If God told you your wayward child would have to go to prison in order for him to become a Christian, you probably wouldn't believe it. If God said you would be single for 10 years because that was when He was going to bring the perfect spouse for you, you probably wouldn't believe it. If God told you the collapse of your business and the loss of all your worldly possessions would bring thousands to Christ, you probably wouldn't believe it. If God told you your spouse walking out the door was the best thing that would ever happen to you, you probably wouldn't believe it.

What God told Habakkuk next shocked him:

> **"For behold, I am raising up the Chaldeans, that fierce and impetuous people who march throughout the earth to seize dwelling places which are not theirs. They are dreaded and feared; their justice and authority originate with themselves. Their horses are swifter than leopards and keener than wolves in the evening. Their horsemen come galloping, their horsemen come from afar; they fly**

like an eagle swooping down to devour. All
of them come for violence. Their horde of
faces moves forward. They collect captives
like sand. They mock at kings and rulers are
a laughing matter to them. They laugh at
every fortress and heap up rubble to capture
it. Then they will sweep through like the
wind and pass on. But they will be held
guilty, they whose strength is their god."
(Habakkuk 1:6-11)

If we were Habakkuk, we would probably have moved out
of the country upon receiving this news. God was raising up a
vicious, violent group of people, the Chaldeans (or Babylonians),
to discipline Israel. Israel had turned away from God, and because
of their disobedience, God would have to do something to get
their attention. He would use an ungodly group of people to
chastise His people. Is that fair, God? Couldn't you just gently
move our hearts back to you? Why this kind of judgment? Don't
you love us?

Habakkuk was starting to get the picture as he responded in
**Habakkuk 1:12 "Are You not from everlasting, O Lord,
my God, my Holy One? We will not die. You, O Lord,
have appointed them to judge; and You, O Rock, have
established them to correct."** Habakkuk was beginning to do
what God wants all of us to do: trust Him. We have to learn to
trust Him with things that seem so wrong. We have to remember
He sees the overall picture, and most of the time, we can't see
what He is doing. Just like Habakkuk, we need to agree He is the
Lord, our God, our Holy One, and our Rock. What He does is
always right.

In Chapter 2, Habakkuk did what most of us need to learn
to do: wait on God. **Habakkuk 2:1** says, **"I will stand on my
guard post and station myself on the rampart; and I will
keep watch to see what He will speak to me, and how I
may reply when I am reproved."** Once he accepted what

God was doing, he waited and listened. Our biggest problem is waiting. We need to know what God is doing now, and when we do not get our answer immediately, we fall apart. That night in Israel, I had to recognize I do not fully understand this fierce battle between these two warring nations. I had to recognize that as sad as the poverty and the children were, God has a plan I'm sure I would not believe if He told me in that moment. I had to go back to the source of everything, which is God, and what He has to say in His Word. Habakkuk responded in this way:

> "I heard and my inward parts trembled, at
> the sound my lips quivered. Decay enters my
> bones, and in my place I tremble. Because
> I must wait quietly for the day of distress,
> for the people to arise who will invade us."
> (Habakkuk 3:16)

Habakkuk was afraid and trembled for what he knew what was going to happen. Could you imagine if you knew that, within a short period of time, your city, state, or country would be invaded? What would you think? What would you do? Would you wait on the Lord? Would you accept what was going to happen? Habakkuk got to the exact point where God wanted me to be that night in the hotel room in Israel.

> "Though the fig tree should not blossom
> and there be no fruit on the vines, though
> the yield of the olive should fail and the
> fields produce no food, though the flock
> should be cut off from the fold and there
> be no cattle in the stalls, yet I will exult in
> the Lord, I will rejoice in the God of my
> salvation. The Lord God is my strength,
> and He has made my feet like hinds' feet,
> and makes me walk on my high places."
> (Habakkuk 3:17-19)

Habakkuk could have fallen apart because things didn't go

as he had hoped or planned. He could have given up on God or stayed mad at Him forever. He could have given up on his faith because he didn't think God was running the Universe like He should. Instead, Habakkuk did what we all need to do: love God and trust Him, regardless of our situation. Whether we are rich or poor, whether we have a job or lose it, we should "exult in the Lord." Whether we are sick or well, we should "exult in the Lord." Whether our spouse walks out on our marriage or we have to be single for 10 more years, we should "exult in the Lord." Whether we have to get food from the shelter to feed our family or we have money to go out to dinner every night, we should "exult in the Lord." Habakkuk learned one thing from seeing bad things going on: God's plans are always right, always just, and always done for a reason.

Our Israel trip taught me how important knowing God's Word is. If you are not reading your Bible on a daily basis, the odds of you falling apart when trouble comes are pretty high. The only way to know someone intimately is to spend time talking to and getting to know them. Likewise, the only way to remotely grasp the ways of God is to see how He dealt with people and nations in the Bible. A sure way to find peace and be comforted in your life is to read accounts of how God dealt with similar situations in past times. We see all the time people who walk away from their faith in Christ because they feel life has treated them unfairly. Often, they have never taken the time to see God is always in control and has a purpose behind everything He does.

Even little brown eyed boys living in Palestine.

# CHAPTER 8

## *Solomon*
## *Discouragement Regarding the*
## *Meaning of Life*

Imagine winning the lottery and having more money than you could ever spend in a lifetime. That, it seems, would be a dream come true. You could buy anything you wanted, build whatever you wanted, and travel wherever you wanted. Wouldn't all your problems be solved? No more late payments on your credit cards. No more working overtime to pay the medical bills. No more stress. Wouldn't that be the best life possible? Probably for a while, but would you have true and lasting happiness?

In the Bible, we are introduced to Solomon, who was known for his incredible wisdom and his unbelievable wealth. Solomon was the son of David and Bathsheba, and when King David died, Solomon took over his throne as the King of Israel. In **1 Kings 3:6-14**, we see Solomon as humble and fearful about the job he had been given. The people of Israel loved his father David, and now Solomon was taking over that position. Instead of asking God for things like money and property, Solomon asked God for only one thing: wisdom to rule the people.

"Then Solomon said, 'You have shown
great lovingkindness to Your servant
David my father, according as he walked
before You in truth and righteousness
and uprightness of heart toward You;
and You have reserved for him this great
lovingkindness, that You have given him
a son to sit on his throne, as it is this day.
Now, O Lord my God, You have made
Your servant king in place of my father
David, yet I am but a little child; I do not
know how to go out or come in. Your
servant is in the midst of Your people
which You have chosen, a great people
who are too many to be numbered
or counted. So give Your servant an
understanding heart to judge Your people
to discern between good and evil. For
who is able to judge this great people of
Yours?' It was pleasing in the sight of the
Lord that Solomon had asked this thing.
God said to him, 'Because you have
asked this thing and have not asked for
yourself long life, nor have asked riches
for yourself, nor have you asked for the
life of your enemies, but have asked
for yourself discernment to understand
justice, behold, I have done according to
your words. Behold, I have given you a
wise and discerning heart, so that there
has been no one like you before you, nor
shall one like you arise after you. I have
also given you what you have not asked,
both riches and honor, so that there will

**not be any among the kings like you
all your days. If you walk in My ways,
keeping My statutes and commandments,
as your father David walked, then I will
prolong your days.'" (1 Kings 3:6-14)**

Because Solomon asked for wisdom, God was pleased
with him and decided to give him wealth and honor also.
In the book of Ecclesiastes, Solomon took a journey that
many people have traveled: one in which he searched for
the meaning of life. What Solomon *thought* he wanted in life
were the very things that kept him on the path of frustration
and discontentment.

Ecclesiastes opens with a phrase that appears often
throughout the book: "Vanity of vanities! All is vanity." What
Solomon recognized on his journey through life was that
the very things he thought would make him happy - wealth,
pleasure, success, fame - were nothing more than vanity. In
the end, they mean nothing. There has to be more to life.

Solomon started with the recognition that life is short.
Generations come and go. The sun rises and sets every day,
and the cycle of life goes on and on. One day, we will all die.
That thought seems depressing, yet when we realize this—
maybe for the first time—it should change our lives. We
should have a sense of urgency to do something meaningful
like helping the less fortunate or spending more time with
our families and less time at the office. Maybe it means
coaching our kids' sports team or just making sure we are
there to watch them play. Maybe it means taking our family
camping or fishing. Maybe it means, just like Solomon
discovered, that day to day work is wearisome, and for all the
time we spend trying to make money, we miss out on the

important things in life. Solomon put it like this:

> "The words of the Preacher, the son
> of David, king in Jerusalem. 'Vanity of
> vanities,' says the Preacher, 'Vanity of
> vanities! All is vanity.' What advantage
> does man have in all his work which he
> does under the sun? A generation goes
> and a generation comes, but the earth
> remains forever. Also, the sun rises and
> the sun sets; and hastening to its place
> it rises there again. Blowing toward the
> south, then turning toward the north, the
> wind continues swirling along; and on
> its circular courses the wind returns. All
> the rivers flow into the sea, yet the sea
> is not full. To the place where the rivers
> flow, there they flow again. All things
> are wearisome; man is not able to tell it.
> The eye is not satisfied with seeing, nor
> is the ear filled with hearing. That which
> has been is that which will be, and that
> which has been done is that which will
> be done. So there is nothing new under
> the sun. Is there anything of which one
> might say, 'See this, it is new'? Already it
> has existed for ages which were before
> us. There is no remembrance of earlier
> things; and also of the later things which
> will occur, there will be for them no
> remembrance among those who will
> come later still." (Ecclesiastes 1:1-11)

Work is absolutely necessary in life. The Bible is clear that we must work hard and not be lazy. In fact, **Proverbs 10:4** says, **"Poor is he who works with a negligent hand, but the hand of the diligent makes rich."** Solomon understood this but also recognized if you put your life into your work and you make work the most important thing, you will never be satisfied. He recognized that someone has done your job before now and will continue on when you are gone. Work is important, but putting undue importance on our jobs will never make us happy and satisfied.

Discouragement can come also in the form of boredom: working every day at a job we hate and wondering why we have to spend the majority of our life doing something we cannot stand to do. Many people we know wake up each morning dreading to go to work. They hate what they do and are just biding their time until they can retire. Is that how life should be? Is that the abundant life God says we can have? Maybe the job you have is the only job you can get, and you have bills to pay.

But think of it this way: if Solomon worked doing exactly what he wanted to and still he wasn't happy, then the work can't really be the problem. We need to recognize the work we do and the job we have are means for giving our lives away. We are to share the gospel with those who need salvation. We are to be a light to those around us, helping those in need and encouraging others. If we are working our eight, ten, twelve hours a day just to fill space in life, then we need to readjust our thinking on work. God has placed you in your workplace for a purpose. Could you start a Bible study once a week in the lunch room? Could you mentor one person and help him or her grow?

Remember this: God has given you passions and desires.

Think of what it is that you would love to do. If you have a desire to do something different, then pray God would open a door somewhere for that to happen. Life is far too short to spend 40 years doing something you hate. My niece just graduated from an online college. She has three children and a hectic life, but pursuing an education was important to her, and she got her diploma. Instead of sitting around being discontent or complaining - do something!! Whether you get your dream job or not, that is never where you will find happiness. True happiness will be felt when you realize where you are is where God wants to use you.

Solomon understood this. He knew work was essential, but he also realized generations come and go. My family has a steel business, and my father started it when I (Lisa) was in high school. To this day, my dad still works there but has passed the presidency of the company down to my brother who in turn has passed it down to his son. Just like Solomon says, generations come and go. Someone has done your job before you and will do it after you are gone so if that is the case, there has to be something more to life than work.

Solomon decided that working was not the key to life, so he decided to pursue pleasure.

> **"I said to myself, 'Come now, I will test you with pleasure. So enjoy yourself.' And behold, it too was futility. I said of laughter, 'It is madness,' and of pleasure, 'What does it accomplish?' I explored with my mind how to stimulate my body with wine while my mind was guiding me wisely, and how to take hold of folly, until I could see what good there is for**

the sons of men to do under heaven the
few years of their lives. I enlarged my
works: I built houses for myself, I planted
vineyards for myself; I made gardens and
parks for myself and I planted in them
all kinds of fruit trees; I made ponds of
water for myself from which to irrigate
a forest of growing trees. I bought male
and female slaves and I had homeborn
slaves. Also I possessed flocks and herds
larger than all who preceded me in
Jerusalem. Also, I collected for myself
silver and gold and the treasure of kings
and provinces. I provided for myself male
and female singers and the pleasures of
men—many concubines. Then I became
great and increased more than all who
preceded me in Jerusalem. My wisdom
also stood by me. All that my eyes
desired I did not refuse them. I did not
withhold my heart from any pleasure, for
my heart was pleased because of all my
labor and this was my reward for all my
labor. Thus I considered all my activities
which my hands had done and the
labor which I had exerted, and behold
all was vanity and striving after wind
and there was no profit under the sun."
(Ecclesiastes 2:1-11)

Solomon figured if working did not bring him happiness,
then he would do everything he could to give himself
pleasure. He had an enormous amount of money, so he drank
the finest wine. He thought building a new house along

with beautiful vineyards, parks, trees and ponds would make him happy. He had people who worked for him, and he had more animals than anyone else. He collected silver and gold and treasures from other countries. He provided himself with women and entertainment. He did not withhold from himself anything that brought him pleasure.

Think about all the things you think would bring you pleasure. Traveling around the world? A new spouse? A new house? New furniture? Shopping sprees with unlimited cash? A new car or boat? How about an RV? The problem is that Solomon was a role model for a life of excess. He had more money than most of us could ever imagine, he denied himself nothing, and in the end, he said it was all vanity. It brought him happiness only for the moment. Material things get old. There are always new styles of clothes, new models of cars and the latest technology to be had. Things wear out and break down and when we look at "things" to make us happy, we will always be discouraged.

We can get very discouraged and depressed trying to fill our lives with everything under the sun to make us happy. Solomon went on and on through Ecclesiastes trying everything he could think of to make himself happy, and after years and years he came to one conclusion: without God, nothing will ever satisfy. **Ecclesiastes 12:13** is Solomon's final conclusion in life, **"The conclusion, when all has been heard, is: fear God and keep His commandments, because this applies to every person."** God's blessings and our satisfaction in life begin and end with Him. Knowing God, having a healthy fear of Him, and doing what He asks us to will bring us joy.

When we put our hope in people or things or vacations

or work, inevitably we will be disappointed. Discouragement comes into our lives when we depend on these things to make us happy. People will disappoint and hurt us. Houses fall apart and need new paint every few years. Vacations end, and we have to go home to the life we left a week earlier. Work is discouraging when the job you spent hours bidding on is given to another company or you are passed up for a promotion.

That is why we have to take our lives and open handedly give them to God for Him to use us however He wants to. That is why Solomon said to keep His commandments. **Matthew 22:37-40** says, **"And [Jesus] said to him, 'You shall love the Lord your God with all your heart, and with all your soul, and with all your mind. This is the great and foremost commandment. The second is like it, You shall love your neighbor as yourself. On these two commandments depend the whole Law and the Prophets.'"**

Discouragement invades our lives when we try to satisfy ourselves with things that do not last. Loving God and loving others will give us meaning in our lives. If you are struggling with life, feeling like nothing is ever satisfying, then take Solomon's advice. Recognize that nothing will ever satisfy you until you surrender your life to the One who gave you life. He saved you for a purpose, and that purpose never means living for yourself to attain worldly pleasures and material goods. Solomon's life was "vanity" until he recognized that nothing would satisfy him except a life that honors God.

# CHAPTER 9

## *Discouragement - We All Need a Friend*

Do you have a friend? Not just an acquaintance but a true friend you know you can talk to about anything? Life can be discouraging, and without someone by your side, praying for you and lifting you up in times of need, it is easy to get stuck in a rut. In an earlier chapter, we spoke of David, a young boy who cared for his family's sheep and was later called by God to become King. God also said something incredible about David: God called him a "man after His own heart." Wouldn't it seem that someone who loved God as much as David did would never get discouraged? Don't people who love God with all their heart trust Him so much that their life never has problems?

Evidently not, since David found himself in a most discouraging situation. **1 Samuel 23:1-2** explains what happened:

> **"Then they told David, saying, 'Behold, the Philistines are fighting against Keilah and are plundering the threshing floors.' So David inquired of the Lord, saying, 'Shall I go and attack these Philistines?' And the Lord said to David, 'Go and attack the Philistines and deliver Keilah.'"**

A great thing about David was that his life was so entwined with God that he didn't want to make a move without knowing if it was what God wanted. How are we doing in this area? Do we make business decisions, financial decisions, or family decisions without consulting God? David knew better, which is probably one reason why God called him a "man after His own heart." David wanted to do the right thing; he wanted to hear from God and then do what he was told. He trusted God to make sure he knew the right answer.

This brings us to an important question: how do we know when we are hearing God's voice? Knowing this seems exceptionally hard because so many other things clutter our minds. We have the world, which bombards us continually, and then we have our flesh that tries to move us to do things against what the Spirit of God is telling us. Fortunately, we have God's Word, the Bible. From cover to cover, God tells us how to live, how to react, and who He really is. Because we have the Holy Spirit living within us, He uses the Bible to convey those truths to us. We have to spend time reading His Word and getting to know Him so that we can distinguish His voice from all the other voices that bombard us daily.

God was telling David to do something very difficult which would probably cost many people their lives. David worried about his men, yet God clearly told him to go to war. But there was a problem: David's men were fearful. **1 Samuel 23:3** says, **"But David's men said to him, 'Behold, we are afraid here in Judah. How much more then if we go to Keilah against the ranks of the Philistines?'"**

Sometimes we are not sure if what we heard from God was right, so we ask again which seems okay to do since David did it in verse 4:

**"Then David inquired of the Lord once more. And the Lord answered him and said, 'Arise, go down to Keilah, for I will give the**

**Philistines into your hand.' So David and
his men went to Keilah and fought with the
Philistines; and he led away their livestock
and struck them with a great slaughter. Thus
David delivered the inhabitants of Keilah."**

The other day I (Lisa) was struggling with this idea of hearing God's voice. I felt the need to talk with someone about an issue, but the opportunity never came up, so I dropped it. Then one day a month or so later, I thought about it again and prayed if this was from God that I would continue to feel this way. I continued to think about it, so a few hours later I wrote this person an e-mail. As soon as I hit the "enter" button, I had a sudden wave of doubt: did I really hear from God? What if it wasn't Him and I just ruined my relationship with this person? What if I wasn't being obedient and really listening? What if, what if, what if?

The questions would not stop going around in my head, so that night I brought up the issue with our small group leader, Bill. He said if I normally walk in the Spirit and want to know what God wants, why would I *not* assume my thought to write an e-mail was from God? He said I needed to believe in faith that I had heard from God because God promises to direct our steps. He also asked a very important question: If it wasn't from God, could He still use it anyway? We know He can and does, so it gave me a peace that I could just trust Him to do with my e-mail whatever He needed to do. As **Proverbs 16:9** says, **"The mind of man plans his way, but the Lord directs his steps."**

The Bible is so important in our lives because we can stand on the promises of God when we feel discouraged about the things we do. When I read a verse like Proverbs 16:9, it made me realize that in my mind I had an idea, but after praying about it, I had to believe that the Lord was directing my steps. It then takes a step of faith for us to act on what we are being told. Remember this though: God will never put in our minds something that contradicts his Word. If you have thoughts of divorcing your spouse and have no Biblical basis for doing so, then those thoughts are not from God. If you are single and have convinced yourself God has told you it is okay to have sex before you are married, you can be sure those thoughts are not from God. If there is a clear command in Scripture against what you are about to do, God would never tell you differently.

We can get so discouraged during the day, questioning every move we make and every choice we make. We need to wake up in the morning and ask God to direct our steps for that day, allowing Him to guide our decisions and thought processes and then do what we think is best. God gave us a brain, and He really does expect us to use it! When we do, instead of feeling discouraged, we should be thankful, knowing He is guiding our mind and our steps. There is a tremendous amount of freedom in knowing He does.

**Psalm 37:31**
> **"The law of his God is in his heart; his steps do not slip."**

**Psalm 37:23**
> **"The steps of a man are established by the Lord, and He delights in his way."**

**Proverbs 20:24**
> **"Man's steps are ordained by the Lord, how then can man understand his way?"**

**Job 31:4**
> **"Does He not see my ways and number all my steps?"**

**Proverbs 4:12**
> **"When you walk, your steps will not be impeded; and if you run, you will not stumble."**

Back to David and his story of discouragement.

**1 Samuel 23:6-15** says,

"Now it came about, when Abiathar the son of Ahimelech fled to David at Keilah, that he came down with an ephod in his hand. When it was told Saul that David had come to Keilah, Saul said, 'God has delivered him into my hand, for he shut himself in by entering a city with double gates and bars.' So Saul summoned all the people for war, to go down to Keilah to besiege David and his men. Now David knew that Saul was plotting evil against him; so he said to Abiathar the priest, 'Bring the ephod here.' Then David said, 'O Lord God of Israel, Your servant has heard for certain that Saul is seeking to come to Keilah to destroy the city on my account. Will the men of Keilah surrender me into his hand? Will Saul come down just as Your servant has heard? O Lord God of Israel, I pray, tell Your servant.' And the Lord said, 'He will come down.' Then David said, 'Will the men of Keilah surrender me and my men into the hand of Saul?' And the Lord said, 'They will surrender you.' Then David and his men, about six hundred, arose and departed from Keilah, and they went wherever they could go. When it was told Saul that David had escaped from Keilah, he gave up the pursuit. David stayed in the wilderness in the strongholds, and remained in the hill country in the wilderness of Ziph. And Saul sought him every day, but God did not deliver him into his hand. Now David became aware that Saul had come out to seek his life while David was in the wilderness of Ziph at Horesh."

Saul was the crazy King who was so jealous and fearful of David taking over his royal position that he was trying to kill him. Day after day, Saul sought out David, which kept David doing two things: running all the time and trusting God to keep him safe. In all the circumstances that seemed so devastating, God never left David's side. We love what verse 15 says: "but God did not deliver [David] into [Saul's] hand." When we are discouraged, it should help us to know God is the author of everything happening in our lives. He is in control, and until He determines something should change, it won't.

We own some land we have been trying to sell for years. It is in a beautiful area in the middle of mountains and desert and it would be a quiet place to live. The funny thing is that it isn't selling. Sometimes I (Rob) can get discouraged, wondering what I am doing wrong. Am I not advertising enough? Is the price too high or too low? Should we build a spec house on the land? All of these questions seem to make me think I am actually in control of this land! As I continue to read God's Word, I am comforted to know that, just as God protected David from Saul, God will protect us from selling this land until His perfect timing. Once I started putting everything we own in His hands, there was no room for discouragement. How can I be discouraged when I don't control the outcome? Maybe God is trying to teach me to trust Him, to sit back, and relax, knowing He alone will bring a buyer at the right time.

Sometimes I get discouraged anyway. Sometimes I feel like I am doing something wrong, and it is *me* who is blocking God's hand in selling this property. Sometimes, even when I know better, I still feel discouraged. It is nice to know even David, a man after God's own heart, felt discouraged at times, and this is why it is important to have a friend—someone you can share your feelings with. David had a best friend named Jonathan who happened to be Saul's son. Jonathan should have been King when his father died, yet he knew God called David to be King. Instead of feeling angry and jealous, Jonathan loved David and was his biggest fan. He went against his own father to defend David. That is true friendship. Here is what Jonathan did for David, according to **1 Samuel 23:16-17**:

> **"And Jonathan, Saul's son, arose and went to David at Horesh, and encouraged him in God. Thus he said to him, 'Do not be afraid, because the hand of Saul my father will not find you, and you will be king over Israel and I will be next to you; and Saul my father knows that also.'"**

Jonathan seemed to know David needed encouragement; running for your life would get exhausting. So Jonathan talked with David and "encouraged him in God." It seems all of us need a Jonathan in our lives—someone who will encourage us and remind us God is still on His throne and He still cares for us. We all need a Jonathan in our lives to remind us God has always been faithful to us and to remind us that, as bad as our circumstances look, God still is working behind the scenes. Evidently, David felt fear since Jonathan told him not to be afraid. David really needed to hear the truth of the situation:

Saul would not find him.
David would be King over Israel.
Jonathan would be right beside him along the way.
Saul knew he would be King, no matter what.

Sometimes we need encouragement like this. We need to know God can still use us even if our marriage failed. We need to know God is still working even if we lose our job. We need to know a broken relationship is still under the control of God. We need to know we don't have to fear the unknown; God is still working upstream. In his book *Second Guessing God*, Brian Jones says this regarding the Israelites who were crossing the Jordan River:

> *As soon as the priests' feet touched the water, God caused the water to stop flowing. In fact, the Bible later tells us that the water stopped*

*completely, the riverbed dried up and God's people were able to cross over on dry ground. Where did God stop the flow of water? Did it stop right where the people were standing? Did the Israelites see God at work with their own eyes? No. The water "piled up in a heap a great distance away, at a town called Adam." (Joshua 3:16)*

*Scholars estimate the town of Adam was roughly nineteen miles upstream from where the Israelites stood, far beyond where they could see. It was a miracle, but it was a miracle the people didn't witness with their own eyes. God performed the miracle upstream, out of their sight.*

*I believe the same situation occurs in our lives today. Here's the powerful truth the children of Israel learned that day: God is always at work upstream in our lives.*

*Where's God? Whenever we face a problem in our lives — sickness, job loss, depression, tragedy or discouragement — God is at work upstream in the situations, beyond our line of sight. The only thing the Israelites could see was the problem right in front of them. They could have concluded that since that raging river was there, God wasn't actively involved in their situation, but they would have been wrong. He was there; they just couldn't see him at work.*[iii]

David was fortunate to have a friend who knew him and loved him. Jonathan knew David well enough to be able to sense his apprehension and fear, and Jonathan came alongside him and encouraged him with the truth. That is why it is so important to read our Bibles and know the truth. If we did not know that God controlled the earthquakes and the snow storms, we would be scared. If we did not know that God moves in the hearts of people or that He alone, through His Spirit, invades peoples' lives and changes them, we would be anxious. If we did not know that God alone is behind the elections and who will win or lose, we would be frightened. When we don't know the truth about who God is and what His character is all about, this world is a scary place to live.

Friends are desperately needed in times of pain and sorrow. People need to know no matter what tragedy has come into their lives, God is still on His throne and in control. We need to be the kind of friend who gives encouragement and hope. We found the perfect example of this in an article written in *People Magazine*. Bill Petit Jr. lost his wife and two daughters in a home invasion in 2007 where he was left for dead in his basement. The last paragraph in this article reminded us how important people are in helping others through tragedy.

*This is the challenge for Bill Petit – to never forget his family but to find a way, somehow to heal. He still wears his wedding ring, regularly attends church and stays close to his daughters' friends, who have reached out to him throughout the year. "If he's having a hard day, we e-mail or text him and tell him we're with him and to be strong," says Kathryn Thompson, 12. The support he has received, he has said, has been "the light" during the dark, dark place he's been in since their deaths. "My faith has been severely challenged, and you may not know it, but you all have pulled me up and kept me afloat."*[iv]

That is what friends do: they keep us afloat when we feel like we're drowning. They remind us our faith in God is still true, even when the darkness surrounds us. They remind us God still loves us and He still has a plan for us. They build us up when we feel down. They encourage us to keep moving forward.

Not only do we need to *have* a true friend, but we also need to *be* a true friend. Most people do not have one good friend to talk to, and most of it boils down to the fact that we don't trust people. If I tell you my innermost thoughts, fears, and dreams, what will you do with them? This is especially difficult in the Church, the one place it should be the easiest. Isn't it easy to let people know about someone else's problems all under the guise of "we need to pray for so and so – he is struggling with…"? True friendship refuses to gossip, true friendship allows for complete honesty, and true friendship affords the encouragement needed for the moment.

The sad part is we have bought into the idea that everyone gossips, even though that is not true. Somehow we hesitate to share our lives for fear the whole world will know all our inner thoughts and hurts. Everyone needs a safe place to be able to vent feelings and emotions, and we need to begin with ourselves. Am I a good friend? Do I listen and then keep my mouth shut? Can people trust me when they talk to me?

A true friend helps to take away the discouragement life can bring, just by being there and listening. Sometimes, that is all we need. To find a true friend, first be a true friend, just like Jonathan. We all need to be "encouraged in the Lord" during our lifetime, and the sooner you find a true friend, the easier life will become.

# CHAPTER 10

## *Moving Out of Discouragement*

We are not immune to discouragement. Many Christians tend to hold their feelings in, without ever talking about them, and we fall deeper and deeper into a dark hole. We are fearful that people will think we are not "spiritual" if we ever question our faith, so we put on a happy face as we walk through the day, and inside we feel like we are dying. Many Christians can be so judgmental, and for fear of what others will think of us, we feel the need to act like nothing is wrong. The Church is the one place we should be able to turn to, yet for many, that is the last place they go.

In order to get out of our discouragement and depression we have to hold on to a few truths. If we forget them, we will continue to live a life of despair.

**God is in control.**

We have to recognize that God is sovereign and in control of all of our circumstances. He is there when you don't feel His presence, and He is there working "upstream" when you feel like things are falling apart. We have to hold on to the fact no matter what our circumstances are in life, God promises this in **Romans 8:28, "And we know that God causes all things to work**

**together for good to those who love God, to those who are called according to His purpose."** Notice what this verse says: God causes all things to work together for good. The one catch to this verse is that He does this for those who love Him. If you are reading this and you are not a Christian, then you cannot claim His promise that He is working together everything in your life for good.

We have to be prepared in life for circumstances to change. Businesses fail, hurricanes destroy lives, people get sick and die, and jobs are lost on a daily basis. But as Christians, we do not need to fall apart when things happen because we have a promise from the God of the Universe that regardless of how it seems, He is making all things work for good.

I (Lisa) just finished reading a book called *Mistaken Identity,* a story about two girls who were in a horrific car accident. One of the girls, Whitney, was thrown 50 feet out of the van and lived, while the other girl, Laura, died. Next to Whitney was a purse belonging to Laura, but since they both had similar hair and body types, the authorities assumed Whitney was Laura. Through a long series of circumstances, the police told Whitney's parents she had died, and Laura's parents spent 5 weeks in the hospital with Whitney who they assumed was their daughter Laura.

Both families were strong Christians, and when they realized that Whitney was not Laura, each family had to deal with some serious emotions. Whitney's parents had buried her five weeks before, and now they realized their daughter was alive and they buried someone else's child. Laura's parents, who had been so thankful their daughter lived through the crash, had to come to terms with the fact their daughter died in the accident. As Christians, they had to hold on to the fact that all things work together for good.

Whitney had a serious head injury, and as she slowly recovered, she realized she would never be the same as she was before. However, she also knew God was in control. Whitney said this:

*Since the accident, and since the mix-up with Laura and me, so many people have heard and seen God's love that wouldn't have heard it any other way. People wrote into the blog, telling how they had become Christians because of this story. Other people became Christians at my funeral and at Laura's. Don said that's what all the people in the van would have wanted, no matter what the cost. Hearing him say that helps me realize God can work through anything, good or bad.*[v]

Because of the media coverage regarding this story and the funerals for these two girls, many people came to Christ. People were able to see the peace God had bestowed on these families. God used this tragic and difficult situation to bring others to Himself and show what true love and forgiveness mean. He worked all things for good.

On a human level, all we can see in this story is heartache, hurt, and sadness. As Christians we have to start looking at life from an eternal viewpoint and not an earthly one. In the scheme of eternity, Laura is home with the Lord and happier now than she ever could be here on earth. People who would have spent eternity in hell separated from God are now going to spend eternity in heaven because of this situation. The parents on both sides were able to write a book that will help many people deal with heartache in their own lives. God is honored through tragedy: He worked all things for good.

That is the main thing we have to come to terms with: God is working behind the scenes in all our situations. We have to learn to trust Him. **Psalm 56:11** says, **"In God I have put my trust, I shall not be afraid. What can man do to me?"** We have to learn to hold onto the hope He has to offer. Many times things do not work out in the way we would like them to, yet when we know God has allowed something into our life for a purpose, it gives us the opportunity to trust in His goodness, knowing He is moving us to a different place in our lives. It is not always easy, but if something bad happened in our lives without the knowledge God was in control, that would be the more difficult place to be. He offers peace to those who know Him, and we cannot let go of the fact that we are *never* out of His control.

Many people have a false sense of who God is. If you happened to be raised in a church in which God was portrayed as harsh and mean, then you will be fearful of Him. If you were raised in a church where you were taught He is all loving and kind and just wants to make you happy, then you will assume He must meet your every desire. The problem is the God most of us imagine in our minds is not the God of the Bible. That is why we put such an emphasis on teaching people the importance of being in God's Word daily.

God is awesome in every way, and He is the Creator and ruler of this world and universe. He loves us incredibly and has given the life of His Son Jesus to prove it. He has given us the history of how He dealt with His chosen people Israel and how He has promised to preserve them forever. He is in control of the past, the present, and the future. All we have to do is open the Bible to see how it all began, and we can read the last book of the Bible to see how it will all end. He controls people and circumstances. He controls earthquakes, tornados, and tsunamis. He is a God who controls everything, which means He cares about everything in our lives.

What He wants us to know is that nothing happens that He does not allow - even the bad things. The Bible says in **Isaiah 45:7, "The One forming light and creating darkness, causing well-being and creating calamity; I am the Lord who does all these."** If we pray for a certain job, that does not mean we will get it. If we pray for a baby, that does not mean we will get one. If we pray for someone who is sick, that does not mean they will get better. Many times God does answer our prayers how we hope, and at other times, He has a different plan. Many people walk away from God because He does not answer a prayer in the manner they expect Him to, but when we begin to understand Him as the Bible portrays Him, we will see we are here to serve Him — not the other way around. When we truly grasp the God of the Bible and devote our lives to Him, only then can we move through life with peace, even in the midst of heartache. All through the Bible, great men and women who faced hardship and tragedies devoted their lives to trusting God, no matter what circumstances they had to deal with. That is truly living.

Remember these men and women in the Bible:

*Noah was asked to build an ark and was ridiculed by all the people watching.*

*Abraham was asked to move to a distant land away from all he knew.*

*Joseph was betrayed by his brothers and thrown into prison for doing the honorable thing.*

*Moses wandered in the wilderness for 40 years with a group of whining, complaining people.*

*Ruth went to live with her mother-in-law in a foreign land after her husband died.*

*Hannah gave her 3-year-old child up to be raised in the temple after she made a vow to the Lord.*

*David was on the run for his life from King Saul who was jealous of him.*

*Solomon was miserable most of his life because of sin.*

*Elijah wanted to die because of fear and exhaustion.*

*Esther went in front of the King in order to save her people and could have been killed for trying.*

*Job lost his family, wealth, and health before God restored him.*

*John the Baptist was discouraged and doubting in prison as he wondered if Jesus forgot about him.*

*Paul was beaten, stoned, and shipwrecked and yet persevered to the end.*

*Peter had to deal with the fact he denied Jesus three times.*

It is so important to recognize these people are in the Bible! They did not always get what they wanted, and they lived very difficult lives. They had another very important thing in common: they trusted God to lead and guide them, and most of the time they had no idea what God was doing. That is the theme throughout the Bible: trusting Him even when times are hard and the road is tough. We have to learn to trust Him even when things do not go our way. We do not have to be discouraged because we can see from these ordinary men and women in the Bible that God was always faithful to them and He will be faithful to you too.

Trust is a difficult thing. We would never walk up to a complete stranger and ask him or her to watch our children because we could never trust someone we don't know! The path to trusting God is taking the time to get to know Him. Read your Bible daily, and pray about everything that comes into your life. Trust Him to guide you, and even when He seems silent, wait for Him.

When we understand God has not left us here on this planet alone, but has given us the opportunity to live here as His children, we will not be discouraged and depressed when things do not go our way. Our niece is moving back to Phoenix, and her family sold their house in Tucson. The day before the house was to close, the buyers backed out, and it was so devastating because our niece and her family were set on getting to their new home. The next day, another offer came in, and it was for more money. See how quickly life changes? Many times when God says "no," He has something better for us. We have to move through life, clinging to **Proverbs 21:1, "The king's heart is like channels of water in the hand of the Lord; He turns it wherever He wishes."**

We can refuse to be discouraged when things do not go our way, knowing God is the One who changes people's hearts in all situations. When a business deal does not go through for us, we know God could have changed the hearts of the people to give us the work, but since He didn't, we can move on in peace trusting He had a good reason. We always tell our children when they are dating that if someone breaks up with them or they break up with someone else, God is moving their hearts in a different direction. If a school does not accept you, that does not mean it is the school's decision; it means God has moved in their hearts not to accept you because He has a different plan for your life. Isn't that an easy way to live? We do not need to live a life of discouragement when things do not go our way because we have trusted our lives to One who knows where we need to be. Because of that, we can rest assured He will take care of us.

**God will never leave us – regardless of how we feel**.

David was the only man in the Bible whom God called a "man after His own heart," yet time after time, God seemed distant and far away from David. Many of us want the feeling of His presence at all times, yet when we look to godly men of the Bible, we can be reassured even they did not always feel close to God.

For example, the author of **Psalm 10** wrote in verse **1**, **"Why do You stand afar off, O Lord? Why do You hide Yourself in times of trouble?"** Sometimes God seems to hide Himself. We hear people talk about praying and seeking God for an answer and hearing only silence from heaven. Remember, that is normal! If David felt it, then we should not be shaken when we go through the same thing. God will answer us in His timing; our job is to continue to pray and seek Him.

**"How long, O Lord? Will You forget me forever? How long will You hide Your face from me? How long shall I take counsel in my soul, Having sorrow in my heart all the**

day? How long will my enemy be exalted
over me? Consider and answer me, O Lord
my God; Enlighten my eyes, or I will sleep
the sleep of death, And my enemy will say, 'I
have overcome him,' And my adversaries will
rejoice when I am shaken." (Psalm 13:1-4)

"My God, my God, why have You forsaken
me? Far from my deliverance are the words
of my groaning. O my God, I cry by day, but
You do not answer; and by night, but I have
no rest." (Psalm 22:1-2 )

"Turn to me and be gracious to me, for
I am lonely and afflicted. The troubles of
my heart are enlarged; bring me out of my
distresses. Look upon my affliction and my
trouble, and forgive all my sins. Look upon
my enemies, for they are many, and they
hate me with violent hatred." (Psalm 25:16-19)

Even David, this man after God's own heart, at times felt
lonely and afflicted. He was distressed, he had enemies, he cried to
God day and night without answers, and he had no rest. He had
sorrow, his enemies seemed to be winning, and people hated him.
Yet through it all, God was silent. Somehow we feel as Christians
that we should never feel sadness and frustration, but that is why
the Bible is so important in our lives. We can rest in God's silence,
knowing great, godly men and women before us have felt the
same way.

"I have sunk in deep mire, and there is no
foothold; I have come into deep waters, and
a flood overflows me. I am weary with my
crying; my throat is parched; my eyes fail
while I wait for my God." (Psalm 69:2-3)

**"My voice rises to God, and I will cry aloud; my voice rises to God, and He will hear me. In the day of my trouble I sought the Lord; in the night my hand was stretched out without weariness; my soul refused to be comforted." (Psalm 77:1-2)**

Even David felt God was hiding Himself. David felt he had been forgotten by God, he had no rest, and his soul refused to be comforted. David's life was filled with affliction and trouble, and many times he could not feel the presence of God. That should be incredibly comforting to those of us who have had seasons in our lives when God has seemed distant. We have to take by faith the fact God is there, working in our lives and behind the scenes even under difficult circumstances.

Even though David often started out writing in despair, he always came back to standing on the promises of who God is. David had the ability to write his feelings of discouragement out, yet he always ended up back at the place where we all need to be: trusting God and remembering who He truly is. David remembered God has always been faithful. He remembered how God saved him, and he always trusted in His lovingkindness—all in faith, regardless of his feelings.

**Psalm 13:5-6**

**"But I have trusted in Your lovingkindness; my heart shall rejoice in Your salvation. I will sing to the Lord, because He has dealt bountifully with me."**

**Psalm 25:20-21**

**"Yet You are holy, O You who are enthroned upon the praises of Israel. In You our fathers trusted; they trusted and You delivered them. To You they cried out and were delivered; in You they trusted and were not disappointed."**

Psalm 25:20-21

"Guard my soul and deliver me; do not let
me be ashamed, for I take refuge in You. Let
integrity and uprightness preserve me, for I
wait for You."

Psalm 69:30

"I will praise the name of God with song
and magnify Him with thanksgiving."

Psalm 69:35-36

"For God will save Zion and build the cities
of Judah, that they may dwell there and
possess it. The descendants of His servants
will inherit it, and those who love His name
will dwell in it."

Psalm 77:11-15

"I shall remember the deeds of the Lord;
Surely I will remember Your wonders of old.
I will meditate on all Your work and muse
on Your deeds. Your way, O God, is holy;
what god is great like our God? You are the
God who works wonders; you have made
known Your strength among the peoples. You
have by Your power redeemed Your people,
the sons of Jacob and Joseph."

Remembering is the key to avoiding a discouraged, depressed
life. Remember how God has come through for you before.
Remember how He saved someone you never thought would be
saved. Remember how He provided for your needs. Remember
and thank Him. Remember how He delivered people in the
past. Trust Him to deliver you from your discouragement. Wait
for Him to lift this dark cloud from you. Sometimes it happens
overnight, and other times it takes days or weeks. Do not walk
away. Just like David did, look to the future, knowing what God
promised He would do. Persevere to the end. He will come

through in His timing and in His way, and in the end, He will get all the honor and praise He deserves.

Brian Jones wrote this about a time in his life when he felt he was losing his faith:

*One night, in a last ditch effort to salvage whatever remnant of faith I had left, I called a mentor and professor of mine from college and shared my struggle with him.*

*I told him, "My faith in God right now is like a walk on the beach. I've taken off my shoes, and as I stand at the water's edge, the tide has started to roll across my feet. It feels wonderful. Up to this point my spiritual journey has been incredible, but in the last six months doubt has begun to paralyze me. It's like when the water goes back out to the ocean. It is washing away the sand underneath me, and my feet keep sinking lower and lower and lower. If this keeps up, there won't be anything left to stand on."*

*Without hesitation he shot back, "Brian, I have stood where you're standing. I've felt the water cascade across my feet. I know how wonderful that feels. But I've also had the water go back out to sea. I've felt the sand get washed out from underneath my feet."*

*He paused—I think he heard me crying—before he slowly finished, "Brian, listen to me when I say this. When the last grain of sand is finally gone, you're going to discover that you're standing on a rock."*

*That one sentence saved me. That one sentence gave me enough spiritual strength to eventually, over time, rediscover hope, which the Bible beautifully calls "an anchor for the soul, firm and secure." (Hebrews 6:19)*
vi

Just as it was for the great men and women of the Bible, the cure to discouragement and depression is knowing God, trusting Him, and recognizing His control in your life. He promises to never leave us or forsake us, and even when we do not feel His presence, we must know by faith that He is there, working behind the scenes.

Deuteronomy 31:6

> "Be strong and courageous, do not be afraid
> or tremble at them, for the Lord your God is
> the one who goes with you. He will not fail
> you or forsake you."

Hebrews 13:5-6

> "Make sure that your character is free from
> the love of money, being content with what
> you have; for He Himself has said, 'I will
> never desert you, nor will I ever forsake you,'
> so that we confidently say, 'The Lord is my
> helper, I will not be afraid. What will man do
> to me?'"

# CHAPTER 11

# *Discouragement: Is it Medical or Spiritual?*

As we close our discussion of discouragement, we would like to address a serious topic which tends to be controversial in the Church. While reading many books regarding Christian counseling, we kept encountering the idea that all issues in life are rooted in sin. This would mean that if we are sad or depressed, those emotions must be produced by some sin in our lives. We would read things like, "Saul in the Old Testament was bi-polar because of his irrational behavior," and as a result, we assumed that chemical imbalances did not exist. We were convinced if a person was depressed or bi-polar, it was because of sin in his or her life that needed to be dealt with.

That all changed one day as we watched our 9-year-old son trying to do his homework. We kept seeing him erasing what he was writing, and when we questioned him, he said he "had to" do this or something bad was going to happen. We could not understand what he was doing, but this behavior kept getting worse. It started affecting everything in his life: he *had* to touch things a certain number of times, he had to walk a certain way, he had to do certain things because, if he didn't, his mind would tell him something bad was going to happen. As we were dealing with this issue, we realized that our 13-year-old was also having the same problems. He told us his mind would tell him that if he didn't walk around the building a certain way, then we would die in a car crash. We had no idea what this was all about.

We decided to go a Christian counselor to see what was wrong with our boys. He explained it sounded like they had Obsessive Compulsive Disorder (OCD). We had never heard of anything like this before and were told to go to the Children's Hospital Psychiatric Ward and talk to the staff there. Our youngest son was put on medicine, and within one year, the OCD was completely gone. Our older son was not as fortunate. Because we did not know what his condition was, we did not get him help immediately, and his became full blown OCD. We kept thinking he just needed to read his Bible more to diminish these "thoughts" he was having; maybe he needed to go to church more or meet with a youth leader more. What we didn't know was that he couldn't focus long enough to even read ten verses in the Bible; his mind would not allow that to happen.

One night, our son was exhausted from his "thoughts" and had convinced himself he would never be able to live a normal life. It was then that Rob said it was time to get some serious help. We talked the next day to a Christian psychologist who gave us the name of a doctor who specializes in OCD. She put our son on medicine, and within three months, these "thoughts" started to subside. He was not worrying like he had been, and his life became normal again. He met a wonderful girl and is now married. ***Thank you, God, for doctors and medicine!***

We have seven children, four of whom are on medication for some type of disorder. The doctor said that something in our genetic makeup produces these issues in our kids. It is amazing to see the difference in our children's lives when they are taking their medicine. They can smile again, and they can focus on reading God's Word, which in turn helps them to grow in their faith. No longer do we assume every mental or emotional issue stems from sin, for God has given us four shining examples to prove to us otherwise.

Let's look at another example. We have a friend who has cancer, and the hardest part for her in the beginning was all the medicine she had to take. The medicine threw her into a deep, dark, black hole that she couldn't seem to get out of. The medicine was helping her get well physically, but the opposite was happening to her spiritually. The more medicine she took, the further she felt from God. Was she actually further from God? No, but the medicine was changing her capacity to think rationally. She had a physical, chemical problem, not a spiritual problem.

As a result of our experiences with our children and our friend, we now look at depression and discouragement a little bit differently. If you feel sad or depressed or experience increased mood swings, you might need to consult a medical doctor. Discouragement can be brought on by many things: busyness, stress, loss of a job, loss of a spouse, or just living life on this earth. Discouragement can be brought on when tragedy strikes, the kids are fighting, or you are just exhausted. Sometimes we don't even know why we are discouraged, but if you consistently feel a dark sense of sadness, please see a physician to see if this could be a medical issue.

We have physical bodies which have physical problems which need to be dealt with in physical manners. **1 Timothy 5:23** says, **"No longer drink water exclusively, but use a little wine for the sake of your stomach and your frequent ailments."** Paul told Timothy to drink wine for his stomach issues because he had a physical problem. In the area of discouragement, we first need to determine whether there is a physical problem. Are you eating properly? Are you getting enough exercise? Are you getting enough sleep?

Certain kinds of chocolate affect me (Lisa) in a seriously negative way. I love the thin mint chocolate Girl Scout Cookies that are sold every year, but immediately after eating them, I become cranky, grouchy, and sad. Something in these cookies gives me incredible mood swings, so now when I am grouchy to my kids, they immediately ask me if I have eaten Girl Scout

Cookies! The other night I came home after an emotional day, the kids seemed to fight more than normal, and I couldn't put my finger on what was wrong with me. I felt that dark cloud of discouragement (physical) which always makes me feel like God is mad at me (spiritual). I was incredibly short with the kids as I put them to bed, and as I walked out of our daughter's room she asked me if I had any Girl Scout Cookies today. I don't normally talk to my kids this way, but I said something mean to her as I abruptly walked out of her room. As I went by our youngest son's room, he said to me, "Mom, I really want my old mom back."

Kids are so honest sometimes it hurts. The next morning I went into their rooms and, with tears streaming down my face, apologized for the hurtful things I said to them the night before. Kids are also incredibly forgiving, which I am thankful for. I started thinking about what I had to eat the day before that could have possibly thrown me into this kind of mood swing, and I realized for lunch I had a really big piece of chocolate cake. I wondered if the same kind of chocolate that affects me so adversely was in that cake. Clearly, some of our discouragement can be traced to what we put into our bodies.

Did I sin by treating my children like I did? Absolutely. There was no excuse for talking to them the way I did, so I can't explain my behavior away with, "The chocolate made me do it." The point is that we have to look at what we are doing to our bodies and see if there is a physical reason for reacting to things like we do. My biggest discouragement comes from acting like this and convincing myself God can't possibly love me or He is mad at me. I seem to fall into this discouragement pattern that spirals deeper and deeper. Instead, I need to learn to go to God's Word and see what He thinks about me:

*Jesus loves me more than I can imagine.*

**2 Thessalonians 2:16–17**
**"Now may our Lord Jesus Christ Himself
and God our Father, who has loved us and**

given us eternal comfort and good hope by
grace, comfort and strengthen your hearts in
every good work and word."

*Jesus died on the cross to release me from my sin.*

## Revelation 1:5
"And from Jesus Christ, the faithful witness,
the firstborn of the dead, and the ruler of
the kings of the earth. To Him who loves us
and released us from our sins by His blood."

*Jesus has forgiven me.*

## Romans 4:7
"Blessed are those whose lawless deeds have
been forgiven, and whose sins have been
covered."

*Jesus will use this incident in my life to conform me to His image.*

## Romans 8:29
"For those whom He foreknew, He also
predestined to become conformed to the
image of His Son, so that He would be the
firstborn among many brethren."

*Jesus will teach my children through my sin how to deal
with others.*

## Romans 8:28
"And we know that God causes all things to
work together for good to those who love
God, to those who are called according to
His purpose."

The flip side to this is that many Christians are discouraged,
and it is **not** the result of a medical issue: it truly is a spiritual

issue. If you are not reading God's Word or if you are not bathing yourself in learning God's ways, you could be discouraged because you are not getting an eternal view of your problems. This could be the true source of your discouragement. As Christians, we need to check our own lives and determine whether our discouragement is a medical or a spiritual problem.

We are all responsible for our own actions. We are all responsible for dealing with our own sin. We cannot sin and blame it on chocolate or lack of sleep or busyness. However, those things can contribute to sin, so we need to look at our eating habits, sleep habits, or our busy schedules. If my physical problems are contributing to my sin problems which contribute to my discouragement, then I need to go to the root of the problem. Again, not all problems are spiritual, but checking the physical is a good place to start if you feel discouraged about life a majority of the time. Our part is to be disciplined enough to stay away from the things that harm us physically.

Our hope and prayer for this book is that you will see that very godly men and women who loved and served God diligently had times of sadness, discouragement, and depression in their lives. We hope by seeing these people, you will be encouraged to relax and wait on God. He *will* show up, and just like in the case of Elijah, it might just be in a still, small, whisper.

# Endnotes

i Denny and Leesa Bellesi, *The Kingdom Assignment,* Grand Rapids, MI: Zondervan, 2007, p. 11.

ii John MacArthur, *The MacArthur Study Bible,* Nashville: Thomas Nelson.

iii Brian Jones, *Second Guessing God.* Cincinnati, OH: Standard Publishing, p. 35.

iv Nicole Weisensee Egan, "Making It Through Each Day," *People Magazine,* July 28, 2008, p. 114.

v Don and Susie Van Ryn and Newell, Colleen, and Whitney Creak, *Mistaken Identity.* New York: Howard Books, 2008, p. 257.

vi Brian Jones, *Second Guessing God,* p. 15.

If you have any questions or comments, please e-mail us at:

Lisa@WomensBibleStudy.com
or
robslaizure@gmail.com

Visit us at our website:
ConnectingTheDotsMinistries.com